SERMON OUTLINES

on

Reading for Sunday & Major Festivals

of

ABC

THREE YEARS CYCLE

SERMON OUTLINES

on

Reading for Sunday and Major Festivals

of

ABC

THREE YEARS CYCLE

I. N. Senapati

Tercentenary Publication

2010

Sermon Outlines on Reading for Sunday Festivals of ABC (THREE YEARS CYCLE) — Published by the Rev. Dr. Ashish Amos of the Indian Society for Promoting Christian Knowledge (ISPCK), Post Box 1585, 1654, Madarsa Road, Kashmere Gate, Delhi-110006.

ISBN : 978-81-8465-047-1

Laser typeset and cover design by **ISPCK,** Post Box 1585, 1654, Madarsa Road, Kashmere Gate, Delhi-110006.

Tel: 23866322/23
e-mail: ashish@ispck.org.in • ella@ispck.org.in
website: www.ispck.org.in

Content

Foreword

Let us acknowledge that a large a number of our Pastors do no prepare their Sermons in a proper manner. The reasons given may vary from person to person. Either they do not have time, or they do not have resource materials or they are lazy. Some have justified by saying that they depend solely on the Holy Spirit and therefore according to them no external support is needed. What I have found and learnt in my own experience that today our congregations are alert and they are able to see and differentiate the one who prepares and the one who does not. In all traditions Sermons have a very important part in our worship services and liturgy and therefore demands seriousness from the one who preaches and also the one who listens. More time should be spent in preparation than preaching. Yes, the guidance of the Holy Spirit is of paramount importance both in preparation and also in preaching.

We are all acquainted with the Lectionary in the Church of North India and I believe that the readings given in the Lectionary are used in the worship services in all our churches, small or big, towns or villages. In order to provide sermon resource materials and following this Lectionary we started producing from the year 2004 "Daily Devotional Notes" and from the year 2008 Sermon Resource materials for Three Years Cycle. Now, from 2010 our Pastors and those who are called to preach will have yet another resource material "Sermon Outlines" prepared by one of our senior Presbyters of the Diocese of Sambalpur.

I have gone through the Sermon Outlines prepared by the Rev. Dr. I.N. Senapati and I have found it very simple and useful for those who love to prepare the Sermon. The pastors of this generation and the generations to come will ever remain grateful to Dr. Senapati for this resource material. I also acknowledge the contribution of the ISPCK in helping us publish all the above three Resource Materials for the benefit of our pastors and lay leaders.

With gratitude to God and with great appreciation to Dr. Senapati I commend this book **"Sermon Outlines"** to our pastors.

Rev. Dr. Enos Das Pradhan
General Secretary
Church of North India

" Thou hast multiplied, O Lord God, Thy wonderous deeds and thy thoughts towards us; none can compare with Thee!

Were I to proclaim and tell of them, they would be more than can be numbered."
(Ps.40:5)
RSV

"Go therefore and make disciples of all nations, baptizing them in the name of the Father and of the Son and of the Holy Spirit, teaching them to observe all that I have commanded you; and Lo, I am with you always, to the close of the age".

(Mt.28 :19-20)
RSV

Preface

I take it as a privilege to write a few lines for the ABC Three Years Cycle Sermon Outlines for the Church of North India and other churches in India and elsewhere, prepared by Revd. Dr. I. N. Senapati. It is an outcome of his sincere and hard labour. Nevertheless, it is the gem of his thirty years' pastoral and pulpit ministry in the Diocese of Sambalpur (CNI). We have lived together and have served together, and so I know, how seriously he prepares and preaches his sermons.

To his credit, Revd. Dr. Senapati has written and published many Christian books and articles in Oriya and English. *Upasana Sahachara, Christa Dharma Tatwa Saara, Gita Sanghita Gita (Psalms in Songs)* Vol. I and II, *Dibya Jyoti* – monthly magazine in Oriya for five years with Bible Studies, Sermon Outlines, Bible Quizes, Health tips and timely Christian articles, a book-let on Christian Faith, Prayers and Worship in Oriya, and the *Vishwa Parivar,* Vol.I and II – series of multilingual Journals on Interfaith Understanding and Dialogue. He has translated the CNI Constitutions and some Evangelism Workbooks into Oriya. He has written many Christian articles for Oriya and English Christian Magazines, and for some Oriya Daily News Papers. Among his unpublished books are the *Commentary on Romans* and Shree Jishu Brutanta (*Gospel Songs), and the Liturgy for the Lord's Supper (CNI)* in Oriya; and answers to the 666 Question raised in the book, *Problem in Paradise* by Dr.Umesh Patri in English. As has been said by Joseph Stalin, Revd. Dr Senapati, as "a *writer is an engineer of the living soul*".

These 195 Sermon Outlines cover Sermons for all Sundays and the Major Festivals following the ABC Three Years Cycle. These have been prepared in clear sentences to avoid ambiguity and to bring about clarity. I believe that as we use these outlines in the preparation of our sermons and proclaim the messages from the Word of God, both the preacher and the listeners may be enriched with the knowledge and wisdom of God, be renewed and revived spiritually, and be strengthened in the mission entrusted to us in obedience to the Divine call and commission, received from our Lord and Savior Jesus Christ, the Rock of our salvation. As the Lord said,

> *"For as the rain and the snow come down from the heaven,*
> *And return not thither but water the earth,*
> *Making it bring forth and sprout,*
> *Giving seed to the sower, and bread to the eater;*
>
> *So shall my Word be that goes forth from my mouth,*
> *It shall not return to me empty, But*
> *It shall accomplish that which I purpose,"*
> *And prosper in the thing for which I send it. Amen !*

(Isaiah 55.10-11/ RSV/ 1946)

+ Rt. Revd. Dr. C. K. Das,
Bishop, Diocese of Sambalpur
Church of North India
Mission Compound,
Bolangir - 767 001
Orissa

Introduction

The Lord God Almighty may be praised and glorified for ever and ever. It is a great joy for me to praise God on completion of the Sermon Outlines for Sundays and Major Festivals according to the Three Years Cycle of A, B and C. After the completion of the commentary on the St.Paul's Epistles to the Romans in Oriya, the Lord had led me to write this book and to computerize it. As I had prepared many sermon outlines and published *Dibya Jyoti* for five years regularly and had often prepared sermon outlines for our Diocese in the past, it was not very difficult for me. But I praise God that He gave me this burden, so that it may be useful for the pastors and preachers of the mainline churches and others in India and elsewhere.

Care has been taken to refer to all four or more scripture portions as prescribed in the Three-Year Cycle system, the names of the books have been cited in brief, and the outlines have been prepared giving some details referring to other related scripture portions on the subjects. Sundays, Major Festivals, Scripture Reading, Themes, etc have been faithfully followed from the ABC cycle. Sermon outlines for different Saints' Day and those for some minor festivals are not included in this book.

Sermon Outlines (C) for the Lenten period up to Easter for Feb-Apr. 2007 have been sent to some CNI Bishops and Pastors for field tests, inviting their kind and valid comments and suggestions for any alterations and improvements. While some sermon outlines are already available, and we are used to making our own sermons very well, I hope and believe that this humble work of these 195 sermon outlines for the Three Years ABC lectionary system may be helpful towards the development of our Christian life and witness in the process of the establishment of the kingdom of God through Jesus Christ our Lord and Saviour. Amen!

June 4, 2007

– **Revd. Dr. I. N. Senapati**

CHAPTER ONE

Sermon Outlines
for YEAR A (1-66)

SERMON NO.1/A-1

Fourth Sunday Before Christmas (Advent I)

M/EW *Scripture Readings:*

Ps 96   Rom 13.11-14

Is 2.2-4   Mt 25.1-1

Theme: Be prepared at all times for the Lord's appearing

Sermon Outline:

1. The Lord Jesus Christ is coming back to judge in righteousness and equity. (Is 2.3-4; Ps 96.10,13)

2. The Lord is coming back soon at any time. (Mt 25.13; Rev.22.7)

3. Many people shall come to praise and worship him as he alone is the Lord of salvation. (Is 2.3; Ps 96)

4. Let us remain prepared for the Day of the Lord putting on Christ and his armours of light to meet him. (Rom 13.11-14; Am 4.12; Eph 5.6-14)

   Amen!

SERMON NO. 2/A-2

Third Sunday Before Christmas (Advent II)

M/EW   *Scripture Readings:*
                    Ps 107.1 -22   Rom 15.4-13
                    Is 40.1-11   Lk 4.16 – 21

Theme: Through the Holy Scriptures God gives us encouragement and hope

Sermon Outline:

1. God's promises of hope are recorded in the Holy Bible. (Ps 107 .1 -22; Is. 40.1-11; 9.1-7; 11.1-12; 60.1-66; etc)

2. In fulfillment of His promises God sent Jesus Christ into the world as the good shepherd and saviour Lord. (Is 40. 8-11; Lk 4. 16-21; Ezk 34; Jn 10; Ps 23)

3. In Christ there is hope for the Jews and the Gentiles, and for the whole world. (Rom 15. 4-13; Mt 11.28-30; Jn 3.16; Eph 1.9-10; Rev 2.10; 3.19-22;21.5)

4. Let us wish one another to avail the eternal joy and peace in Christ according to the promises of God in the scriptures. Amen! (Rom. 15.13; Jn. 1.12-13; 3.16; Ps. 110.4)

SERMON NO. 3/A -3

Secondary Sunday Before Christmas (Advent III)

M/EW   *Scripture Readings:*
                    Ps 72   1 Cor 4.1-5
                    Is 11.12   Mt 3.1-12

Theme: John the Baptist – A model for Christian ministers

Sermon Outline:

1. Life and work of John the Baptist (Mt 3.1-12; Is. 40. 1-8).

2. John's prophecy about Jesus (Mt 3.11-12; Is. 11.1-9).

3. John's exemplary life and ministry – humble and bold. (Mt 3. 1-10; 10.2-19; Jn 1.26-27)

4. Let us pray for all God's servants for appropriate life style and ministry. (Mt 26.41; 10.16-39) Amen!

SERMON NO. 4/A-4

The Sunday Berfore Christmas (Advent IV)

M/EW   *Scripture Readings:*

Ps 89   Gal 4.1-7

Is 7.1-16   Mt 1.18-25

Theme: Mary's Son is Emmanuel – God with us

Sermon Outline:

1. Joseph and Mary – God's chosen couple (Mt 1.18-25)

2. Jesus, the Emmanuel – the promised Messiah and eternal King. (Is 7. 1-16; Mt 1.23; 28.20; Ps 98.1-4, 19-29)

3. The grace of Divine Sonship to be shared in Christ Jesus (Gal 4.1-7; Rom 8.15-17; Jn 1.12-13)

4. Let us praise God for Jesus, the Lord Emmanuel, and invite him to our life and work. (Ps. 89.1-4)   Amen!

SERMON NO.5/A-5

The Christmas Day

M/EW   *Scripture Readings:*

Ps 98   Heb 1.1-12

Mic 5. 2-4   Jn 1.1-14

Theme: The birth of the saviour, who is the Word made flesh

Sermon Outline:

1. Jesus, the promised Messiah of Bethlehem. (Mic 5.2-4; Lk 2. 1-16)

2. Jesus, the Word made flesh is the Son Of God.
    (Jn 1.1-18; Heb1.1-12)

3. The Saviour Lord is the king for ever. (Heb 1. 6-12)

4. Let us sing new songs with the angels, praising God for
    the new life, peace and salvation available in Christ. (Ps
    98; Lk 2.14) Amen!

SERMON NO. 6/A -6

First Sunday After Christmas

M/EW   *Scripture Readings:*
                Ps 128   Col 3.12-12
                Zech 8.3-6   Mt 2 13 -23

Theme: Family Life

Sermon Outline:

1. God's promises of joy and peace in Christ the Lord. (Zech
    8.3-6)

2. Return of happy family life. (Mt 2. 19-23; Ps 128)

3. Put on love and practice peace and harmony in thankful
    hearts to God. (Col 3.12-21)

4. Let us rejoice in the Lord, for he has done great things
    through Christ. (Phil 4.4-7; Lk 1.46-55) Amen!

SERMON NO.7/A -7

The Naming of Jesus
(January 1, the New Year Day)

M/EW   *Scripture Readings:*
                Ps 113   Acts 4.5-12
                Ex 3.1-15   Lk 2. 15-21

Theme: Do everything in the name of the Lord

Sermon Outline:

1. The circumcision and naming of Jesus. (Lk 2.15-21)

2. The powerful name –Jesus (Mt 11.4-5; 1 Jn 1.7; Acts 4.5-12)

3. Praise the saving name of the Lord Jesus Christ, and rejoice in Him. (Ps 113; 117; 118) Amen !

SERMON NO.8/A-8

Second Sunday After Christmas (Epiphany)

M/EW   *Scripture Readings:*
               Ps 103   Eph 1.3-8
               Prov 8.1, 22-31   Jn 1.9-18

Theme: We share in the Sonship of Christ

Sermon Outline:

1. Man is created in the wisdom of God Almighty. (Prov 8)

2. We share the riches of His grace in Christ, His Son and our saviour Lord. (Eph 1.3-8; Phil 4.19)

3. Let us bless the Lord for all His goodness and steadfast love. (Ps 103; Is 135) Amen !

SERMON NO. 9/A-9

Third Sunday After Christmas (Epiphany)

M/EW   *Scripture Readings:*
               Ps 67   Eph 3.1-12
               Is 60. 1-5   Mt 2.1-12

Theme: The coming of the wise men from the East

Sermon Outline:

1. Jesus was born as the Lord and saviour of the whole world. (Ps. 67)

2. Many people shall come to worship him, and shall offer precious gifts at his feet. (Mt 2.1-12; Is 60.1-5)

3. Our duty is to proclaim the message of the mystery and riches in Christ Jesus all over the world (Eph 3.1-12; Mt 28. 15-20) Amen !

SERMON NO.10/A-10

Third Sunday After Christmas (Baptism of Jesus)

M/EW   *Scripture Readings:*

Ps 2   Acts 10. 34-48

Is 42. 1-13   Mt 3.13-17

Theme: *During His Baptism, Jesus was revealed as the Son of God*

Sermon Outline:

1. The Baptism of Jesus. (Mt 3.13-17)

2. Jesus was declared as the beloved Son of God. (Mt 3.17)

3. Jesus was prophesied to be the Messiah, saviour Lord and eternal King. (Ps 2; Heb 1)

4. Jesus was prophesied to be the suffering servant of God, and the saviour of the world. (Is 42; Acts 10. 34-48)

5. Let us celebrate the Divine Sonship and eternal Lordship of our saviour. Amen!

SERMON NO. 11/A -11

Fourth Sunday After Christmas

M/EW   *Scripture Readings:*

Ps 40.1-10   1 Pet 1.13-21

Ex 12.1-8   Jn 1.29-37

Theme: Jesus revealed as the Son of God

Sermon Outline:

1. Jesus is the sacrificial lamb once for all. (Ex. 12.1-8; Heb 9.11-28)

2. Jesus on the cross takes away the sins of the world. (Jn 1.29; 1Pet 1. 18-20)

3. Blessed is the man who trusts in Jesus the Lord and saviour. (Ps 40.4; 1 Pet 2.9-10; Rom 13.10)

4. Let us sing new songs in praising God for our gracious saviour, and proclaim His deliverance. (Ps 40.1-3, 9-10) Amen!

SERMON NO. 12/A -12

Fifth Sunday After Christmas

M/EW   *Scripture Readings:*
                Ps 27   Col 1.1-14
                Job 3.1-10   Mt 4.12-17,23-25

Theme: Jesus has brought us out of darkness to light

Sermon Outline:

1. Due to the trials by Satan, Job's life became full of darkness and sorrows. (Job 3.1-10)

2. Jesus has overcome Satan, and can free us from the power of darkness and sorrows. (Mt 4.1-17, 23-25)

3. Jesus is the great light, whosever believes and follows him shall not walk in darkness. (Mt 4.16; Jn 8.12; Col. 1-14; Eph 5.7-10) Amen

SERMON NO. 13/A-13

Sixth Sunday after Christmas

M/EW   *Scripture Readings:*

Ps 126   1 Thes 2.1=12

Amos 3.1-8   Mark 1.14-20

Theme: Jesus calls his disciples to work for the Kingdom of God

Sermon Outline:

1. The kingdom of God is near. (Mk 1.14-15)

2. Jesus calls his twelve disciples to work for his Kingdom (Mk 1. 16-20)

3. Jesus' disciples should proclaim his gospel with full dedication, even in hostile conditions. (1 Thess. 2.1-8; Mt 5.10)

4. Let us pray for Jesus' disciples to be worthy of the Lord and His Kingdom. (1 Thess. 2.9-12; Mt 5.11-12) Amen!

SERMON NO. 14/A-14

Seventh Sunday After Christmas

M/EW   *Scripture Readings:*

Ps 45   Eph 5.21-32

Hos 2.16-20   Jn 3.25-36

Theme: Christ is the Bridegroom of the Church

Sermon Outline:

1. The prophecy of the Bride and the Bridegroom. (Hosea 2.16-20)

2. The prophecy was fulfilled in the Lord Jesus Christ. (Jn 3.25-36)

3. The loving relationship between the Lord and the Church, the Bride. (Ps 45; Eph 5.21-32)

4. Let us pray constantly, as the Bride of the Lord under preparation. (Rev 19.5-8; 21.5; Philp 1.9-11) Amen!

SERMON NO.15/A -15

Eighth Sunday After Christmas

M/EW   *Same as 24ᵗʰ/ 25ᵗʰ Sunday after Pentecost*

SERMON NO 16/A-16

Ninth Sunday Before Easter

M/EW   *Scripture Readings:*

Ps 104. 1-30   *Col 1. 15-20*

Gen 1.1-5, 26-31   *Jn 1.1-13*

Theme: God creates and redeems all things through Christ

Sermon Outline:

1. God created the world with his creative Word, who is Christ. (Gen 1.1-31; Jn 1.1-14; Heb 11.3)

2. God also recreates, redeems and reconciles all things with himself in Christ (Jn 1.12-13; Col 1 .14-20; Eph 1.9.10)

3. Let us praise God for his wonderful deeds of redemption in Christ.Amen!

SERMON NO. 17/A-17

Eighth Sunday Before Easter

M/EW   *Scripture Readings:*

Ps 51.1-17   *Rom 1.18-25*

Is   *Mt 13.10-17*

Theme: Our sins begin with refusing to hear God

Sermon Outline:

1. Man is a sinner by birth (Ps 51.5; Gen3; Rom 3.10, 23)

2. Refusing to hear God adds further sins, and leads us to the eternal hell fire (Is 1.1-9; Mt 13.10-17; Rom 1.18-25; Heb 3.7-11)

3. Hearing the Word of God humbly leads to repentance and forgiveness of sins. (Mt 13.17; Ps. 51.17; Rom 10.17; Acts 2.41;Jn 1,12-13)

4. Let us listen to His words, repent, so that we may be forgiven. Amen!

SERMON NO.18/A -18

Seventh Sunday Before Easter

M/EW   *Scripture Readings:*
Ps 100   1 Tim 2.1-7
Is 56.3-8   Mt 8.5-13

Theme: It is God's will that all people should be saved

Sermon Outline:

1 God invites openly all the people to believe in him and be saved. (Ps 100; Mt 11.28-30; Jn 3.16)

2. The Lord Jesus heard the prayer of the Gentile believer (Mt 8.5-13; Acts 10)

3. God wishes to save everyone, and he does not wish that anyone should perish. (Is 56. 3-8; 1 Tim 2.1-7; 2 Pet 3.9)

4. Let us praise God for His Grace and loving kindness. (Acts 15.11; Rom 6.23) Amen!

SERMON NO.19/A-19

Ash Wednesday

M/EW   *Scripture Readings:*
Ps 38   1 Cor 9.24-27
Is 58   Mt 6.1-6, 16-18

Theme: The spirit of Christian discipline (sadhana)

Sermon Outline:

1. True repentance is acceptable to the Lord. (Ps. 38; Is 58. 1-9a; Jer. 15.19)

2. Paul's exemplary humility and self-control. (1 Cor 9.24-27)

3. Jesus' teaching on humble prayers and private fasting. (Mt 6.1-6, 16-18)

4. Let us come before the throne of grace with confidence, humility and repentance. (1 Pet. 5.6-7; 2 Chr 7.14) Amen!

SERMON NO. 20/A-20

Sixth Sunday Before Easter

M/EW   *Scripture Readings:*

Ps 91   1 Cor 10.6-13

Deut 8.1-5   Mt 4. 1-11

Theme: God's word gives us strength to resist temptation

Sermon Outline:

1   God's promising words of grace and security are incomparable. (Ps 91)

2. God, sometimes, allows temptations to strengthen our faith and trust in him. (Deut 8.1-5; 1 Cor 1.6-13; Rev 3.19-22)

3. The Lord Jesus himself overcame the temptations of the Devil by the word of God. (Mt 4.1-11; Is 40.8;2 Tim 3.16-17)

4. Let us trust in God and his word and overcome temptations. Amen!

SERMON NO.21/A-21

Fifth Sunday Before Easter

M/EW   *Scripture Readings:*

                Ps 42   1 Cor 10.1-5

                Ex 17.1-7   Jn 4.5-42

Theme: Christ gives the living water of the Spirit

Sermon Outline:

1 God provided heavenly water from the rock in the wilderness. (Ex 17.1-7; 1 Cor 10. 1-5)

2. Jesus Christ revealed before the Samaritan woman that he is the source of the living water. (Jn 4.14; Jer 2.13)

3. Let us praise God for His free offer of the living water in Christ. (Ps 42.1-2; Is 55.1-2) Amen!

SERMON NO. 22/A -22

Fourth Sunday Before Easter

M/EW   *Scripture Readings*

                Ps 43   Eph 5.8-14

                Ex 13.17-22   Jn 9.1-41

Theme: Christ in the Light of the world

Sermon Outline:

1. God is light, and He is the creator and the master of light, both physical and spiritual (Jn 1.5; Gen 1.3; 13.17-22; Jn 1.4-5; Ps 43.3)

2. God's light stands for truth (Ps.43.3) and life. (Jn 1.4-5)

3. Jesus Christ declared that he is the light of the world, and his disciples should also walk in the light. (Jn 8.12; Eph 5.8-14; Mt 5.14)

4. Jesus gave light in the eyes of the blind man (Jn 9) and life to Lazarus. (Jn 11)

5. Let us pray that the Lord may lead us in the path of truth and the celestial light. (Ps 43.3-4) Amen!

SERMON NO.23/A -23
Third Sunday Before Easter

M/EW   *Scripture Readings:*

Ps 36   Rom 14. 7-9

1 King   Jn 11.1-44

Theme: Christ is the resurrection and life

Sermon Outline:

1   God gave life to the dead child of Zarephath. (1 King 17.17-24)

2. Jesus Christ gave life to Lazarus. (Jn 11)

3. Jesus Christ is the Lord of Life. (Rom 14.7-9)

4. Jesus Christ demonstrated that he is the resurrection and life. (Jn 11.25)

5. Let us praise God and pray that we may share the resurrection and eternal life in Christ. Amen!

SERMON NO.24/A-24
Second Sunday Before Easter

M/EW   *Scripture Readings:*

Ps 89.34-51   2 Cor 5.11-19

Is 50.4-10   Jn 11.45-53

Theme: The meaning of the death of Christ

Sermon Outline:

1   Christ was humiliated persecuted as King David. (Ps 89.34-51; Is 50.4-10)

2. Christ died for all, so that all may die and live with him. (2 Cor 5.11-19; Rom 4 24-25; 6.4-5)

3. Those who believe and trust in him shall have eternal life. (Jn 11.45-53)

4. Let us pray that the death of Christ may be meaningful and a blessing to us, and to his followers. (Is. 53.54; Rom.3, 6) Amen!

SERMON NO. 25/A-25

The Sunday Before Easter in the Passion Week of Christ
(*Palm Sunday*)

M/EW   *Scripture Readings:*

Ps 24   Philip 2.5-11

Zech 9.9-12   Mt 26. 1-2766,

                              or 27.11-54

Theme: Christ enters Jerusalem to offer his life for the salvation of the world

Sermon Outline:

1. Apart from the Almighty and Holy God no one can enter into his Heavenly city of God. (Ps 24)

2. Christ's entry into Jerusalem on the back of a colt was a messianic fulfillment of his eternal kingship as the Son of David. (Zech 9.9-12)

3. At the cost of his sufferings and death on the cross Christ has triumphantly been exalted to the right hand of the father in Heaven. (Philp 2.5-11; Mt 26,27)

4. Let us rededicate ourselves at the feet of the Lord Jesus to receive salvation and to live with him in heaven. (Jn 14. 1-6; Ps. 23.6; Rev 2.10; 3.19-22) Amen !

SERMON NO.26/A-26

Monday Before Easter in the Passion Week of Christ

M/EW   *Scripture Readings:*

Ps 27.2-5, 13-14   Lk 19. 41-48

Is 42. 1-7

Theme: Day of Prayer – Return and be restored, ask and you shall receive

Sermon Outline:

1. Wait upon the Lord in the house of God in prayer. (Ps 27; Lk 19.46)

2. The Lord will bring forth justices, and shall not bruise the weak and righteous. (Is 42.1-7)

3. Let us come to the Lord in humble repentance and confidence, and blessed and restored. (Mt 7.7; 1 Pet 5.6-11) Amen!

SERMON NO, 27/A-27

Tuesday Before Easter in the
Passion / Holy Week

M/EW   *Scripture Readings:*
              Ps 71.1-2,9-12   Mk 14.1-9
              Is 49. 1-7

Theme: Take refuge in the Lord

Sermon Outline:

1. Christ is the Light of the world. (Is 49.1-7)

2. He is the Rock of refuge. (Ps 71.3)

3. He forgives the repentant sinners. (Mk 14.1-9)

4. Let us take refuge in him with repentance and receive forgiveness and redemption. Amen!

SERMON NO. 28/A-28

Wednesday Before Easter

M/EW   *Scripture Readings:*
              Ps. 55 . 12-14; 20-22   Lk 22.1-6
              Is 50.4-1

Theme: *The Betrayal of Jesus*

Sermon Outline:

1. King David was betrayed by his companions. (Ps. 55)

2. The Lord Jesus was betrayed by his disciple, priests and his own people. (Lk 22.1-6)

3. But the righteous are lifted up by the Lord. (Ps 55.16-23; 30.1; 16&56)

4. Bless the Lord, O My soul, for his loving kindness is inconceivable. Amen!

SERMON NO. 29/A -29

Thursday Before Easter
(Monday Thursday)

M/EW   *Scripture Readings:*

Ps.116. 1-2, 12-19   1 Cor 11.23-29

Ex. 12. 1-8, 11 -14   Jn. 13. 1-7, 34-35

or   *or*

Jer.31.31-34   Jn.6.35-39, 47-51

Theme: *Jesus gives his disciples a new commandment, and instituted the Lord's Supper.*

Sermon Outline:

1. The Lord's Supper reflects the new covenant. (Ex. 12.1-14; Jer. 31.31-34; Jn 13. 1-17, 34-35)

2. The Lord's Supper assures eternal life. (Jn 6.35-39, 47-51)

3. The Lord's Supper reminds the love of God and strengthens the mission of proclamation of the Gospel. (1 Cor 11.23-29)

4. Let us confess our sins and share the Lord's grace of eternal life. (1 Jn 1.7; Jn 6.53-54) Amen!

SERMON NO. 30/A -30

Good Friday

M/EW   *Scripture Readings:*
              Ps. 22.1-11, 14-20, 22-28   Heb 10.4-24
              Is. 52.13-53.12   Jn.18.1-19.42
                                                 or 19.1-37

Theme: The victory of the Cross

Sermon Outline:

1   The Holy Father forsake His Son to suffer and die for the world. (Ps 22; Is. 52; Jer. 18,19)

2. Jesus offers himself in fulfillment of the redemptive plan and promises of God. (Heb 10. 4-24; Ps 40. 6-8; Jer 31.31-34)

3. In Jesus' wound, sinners are healed; and in his death they receive eternal life. (Is 52-53; Rom 6.5-6, 6.23; Jn 3.16)

4. Christ's life and mission find victory on the Cross of Calvary. (Jn 18-19; Is 52-53; I Cor 1.18-2.9)

5. Let us praise the Lord will all gratefulness for his redeeming death, and rededicate ourselves at the feet of the Cross of Calvary. Amen!

SERMON NO 31/A -31

Easter Sunday

M/EW   *Scripture Readings*
              Ps 118   Col. 3.1-4
              Ex. 15.1-2, 19-21   Lk. 24.13-35

Theme: The Lord is risen, indeed!

Sermon Outline:

1. Jesus Christ has risen indeed – the event. (Lk. 24)

2. His resurrection signifies his triumph over death. (1 Cor 15.55,57)

3. His resurrection, as the first fruit among the dead, assures resurrection of the faithful. (1 Cor. 15.20-30)

4. His resurrection encourages heavenly life on earth. (Col.3.1-4)

5. Let us believe in the risen Christ and trust in him for all the blessings through him. Amen!

SERMON NO. 32/A -32

First Sunday After Easter

M/EW   *Scripture Readings:*
                Ps 118   Col.3.1-4
                Ex. 15.1-2, 19-21   Lk. 24.13-35

Theme: The Lord is risen indeed!

Sermon Outline:

1. Jesus Christ has risen indeed – the event. (Lk. 24)

2. His resurrection signifies his triumph over death. (1 Cor 15.55, 57)

3. His resurrection, as the first fruit among the dead, assures resurrection encourages heavenly life on earth. (Col.3.1-4)

4. His resurrection encourages heavenly life on earth. (Col.3.1-4)

5. Let us believe in the risen Christ and trust in him for all the blessings through him. Amen!

SERMON NO. 32/A-32

First Sunday After Easter

M/EW   *Scripture Readings:*
                Ps 98 *or* 118. 19-26   1 Pet 1.3-9
                Acts 2.41-47   Jn 20. 19-31

*Theme: Joy and peace, power and new life are given through
          the resurrection of Christ*

Sermon Outline:

1   Rejoice in the risen Lord, as he is the cornerstone of our
    faith. (Ps 118.22; Jn.20.24-29; Pet.2.6-7)

2. Resurrection of the Lord gives us new life and
    hope of the righteous. (1 Pet 1.3; Ps. 118.30-35; 1.5-6;
    16.9-10)

3. The risen Lord assures heavenly peace, power and glory
    now and for ever, after genuine faith and suffering
    (1 Pet 1. 4-7; 5.6-11; Acts 1.8)

4. Let us thank God for the new life and peace in the risen
    Lord Jesus Christ. Amen!

SERMON NO. 33/A-33

Second Sunday After Easter

M/EW   *Scripture Readings:*
                Ps. 30   Acts 2.22-32
                1 Pet. 3.13-18   Lk 24.13-35

Theme: Witnesses to Christ's resurrection

Sermon Outline:

1. Resurrection of the Lord gives joy of eternal life and
    glory in Heaven. (Ps. 30.3-6)

2   The risen Lord gives strength and confidence to witness.
    (Ps. 30.11-12; Acts 2.32)

3. The risen Lord went to the Sheol to proclaim the
    Good News and set a model to witness. (1 Pet.3.18-19)

4. Let us seek the power and grace of the risen Lord to be
    his witnesses. (Lk 24. 13-35; Acts 2.32) Amen!

SERMON NO. 34/A-34

Third Sunday After Easter

M/EW   *Scripture Readings:*

Ps. 23   Acts.2.32-42

1 Pet.2.19-25   Jn 10.1-10

Theme: The Good Shepherd

Sermon Outline:

1   Jesus as the good shepherd gave his life for his sheep. (Jn.10.1-10)

2.   The risen Lord saves the sinners, who repent and receive baptism. (Acts 2.32-41)

3.   He is the guardian of those who believe and trust in him. (1 Pet 2.19-25)

4.   Let us trust in Jesus, the risen Lord and the good shepherd for his loving kindness and care. (Ps 23; Prov.3.5-7) Amen!

SERMON NO.35/A-35

Fourth Sunday After Easter

M/EW   *Scripture Readings:*

Ps .63.1-8   Acts 6.1-7

1 Pet.2.2-10   Jn.14.1-14

Theme: Jesus is the Way, the Truth, and the Life

Sermon Outline:

1.   Jesus guides his servants in the right path. (Jn.14.10-14; Acts 6.3-4)

2.   Jesus is the Messiah in truth, the cornerstone of our faith. (1 Pet 2.6-8; Ps 118.22)

3.   Jesus and his teaching gives new life to his faithful followers. (1 Pet 2. 1-5; Jn 14.1-6)

4.   Let us trust in Jesus, and follow him as he leads us to the Father in heaven for eternal life. Amen!

SERMON NO. 36/A-36

Fifth Sunday After Easter

M/EW   *Scripture Readings:*

Ps. 32   Acts 16.6-10

1 Pet 4.7-11   Jn 14.15-21

Theme: The promises of the Holy Spirit

Sermon Outline:

1. Jesus fulfilled his promise to give the Holy Spirit to his people. (Acts 1.8; Jn. 14.15-21)

2. The Holy Spirit guides and supports the ministry of his servants. (Acts 4. 7-11)

3. The Holy Spirit convicts, intercedes and comforts the people of God. (Ps. 32:5-6; Rev. 8.26-27)

4. Let us come to the Lord through the Holy Spirit and receive his blessings. (Rom 8.26;1 Cor.2.10-13) Amen!

SERMON NO 37/A-37

Ascensions Day

M/EW   *Scripture Readings:*

Ps. 24.7-10 *or* Ps.97   Dan.7.9-14

Acts 1.3-11   Mt.28.16-20

Eph.1.15-23   Lk 24. 44-53

Theme: The son of man is exalted to the right hand of God

Sermon Outline:

1. Jesus Christ ascended to heaven according to the providence of the Father. (Dan.7.9-14)

2. Jesus' ascension proves that his name is greater than all names. (Eph 1.15-23; Phil 2.9-11)

3. Jesus shall come back to take us into heaven. (Acts 1.3-11 Jn.14.1-6; 1 Thess.4.16-18)

4. Let us remain prepared to be accepted by him into heaven. (Ps 24; Mt 25.1-13; Phil 1.9-11; Rev.19.7-8) Amen!

SERMON NO.38/A-38

Sixth Sunday After Easter

M/EW   *Scripture Readings:*
                  Ps .73   1 Pet.4.12-19
                  Acts 1.12-14   Jn.17.1-11

Theme: Christ's ascension is a sign of our glorious destiny

Sermon Outline:

1. A righteous is ambitious of living near God for ever. (Ps.73.28; 23.6)

2. Jesus is gracious enough to keep his beloveds near him for ever. (Jn. 14.1-6; 17.1-11, 26)

3. Jesus shall welcome his obedient followers into his eternal adobe in heaven. (1 Pet 4.12-19; Rev.3.19-22; 20.11-15; Ps.1.5-6)

4. Let us praise God for his gracious plan to admit us for eternal life in heaven through Christ. (Jn.3.16) Amen!

SERMON NO.39/A-39

The Pentecost Sunday

M/EW   *Scripture Readings:*
                  Ps.139   Acts 2.1-31
                  Joel 2.28-32   Jn.20.19-23

Theme: The gift of the Holy Spirit

Sermon Outline:

1. The Day of Pentecost is the Day of the Holy Spirit, according to the promise of God. (Acts 2.1-12; Joel 2.28-30)

2. Jesus gives the gift of the Holy Spirit to his faithful servant's. (Jn.20.19-23; 1 Cor.12.1-11)

3. The Holy Spirit gives comforts, wisdom and power to witnesses. (Acts 2.29-32; 4.13-31)

4. Let us pray for the gifts of the Holy Spirit and be the Lord's witnesses. (Acts 1.8) Amen!

SERMON NO.40/A-40

First Sunday After Pentecost
(The Trinity Sunday)

M/EW   *Scripture Readings:*

Ps 33   Rom.8.11-17

Ex. 6.2-8   Mk. 1.7-15

    or

Gen .1.1-3

Theme: God the Holy Trinity

Sermon Outline:

1. God – the Father, the Son and the Holy Spirit, the Trinity God-head work together. (Gen 1.1-3,26-27; Mk.1.7-15; Lk.1.26-38;3.21-22)

2. The Father, Son and the Holy Sprit are equally Almighty and gracious. (Jn.14; Rom.8; Heb,1,2)

3. The Special ministries of the Trinity:

    (a) God the Father, the Creator and all powerful. (Gen.1, 2)

(b) The Son, Jesus Christ is the Saviour, Redeemer Messiah the Christ. (Jn.3)

(c) The Holy Spirit – The Counselor, Enabler, Comforter and indwelling giver of peace. (Jn 14; 1Cor 12)

4. May God help us to understand and believe in the biblical revelation of the Trinitarian God-head.   Amen!

SERMON NO.41/A-41

Second Sunday After Pentecost

M/EW   *Scripture Readings:*

Ps 119.1-8	2 Cor. 6.3-10
Is.61.1-9	Mt. 5.1-12

Theme: *Jesus tells us, who are truly blessed, Happy*

Sermon Outline:

1. Blessed are those who obey the Lord's commandments and serve the needy. (Ps 119.1-8; Mt.5.1-12)

2. Blessed are those who preach the gospel of salvation by the Power of the Holy Spirit. (Is. 6.1-9)

3. Blessed are those who proclaim the Day of the Lord (2 Cor.1-10)

4. Let us proclaim the Day of the Lord and remain prepared for His blessing and eternal peace. (Am.4.12; Phil 1.9-11)   Amen!

SERMON NO. 42/A-42

Third Sunday After Pentecost

M/EW   *Scripture Readings:*

Ps. 37.1-11	1 Jn.3.11-18
Gen.4.2b-10	Mt.5.17-25

Theme: Our hearts must be kept free from anger and Hatred

Sermon Outline:

1. Cain's anger and hatred brought curse to the family and to others. (Gen.4.2b-10)

2. Offerings with anger and hatred are not acceptable to the Lord. (Mt.5.22-24)

3. Love builds up. (1 Jn.3, 11-18; 1 Cor.8.1; 13.13; Eph.4.11-16)

4. Instead of anger and hatred, let us put on Christ and practice love. (Gal.3.27; Col.3.14; 1Jn.3.18; Jn.15.9, 17) Amen!

SERMON NO.43/A-43

Fourth Sunday After Pentecost

M/EW   *Scripture Readings:*
Ps.34   Eph.4.17-25
Gen.6.5-8   Mt.5.27-37

*Theme: **The sources of truth and purity is in the heart***

Sermon Outline:

1. Sin corrupts the human heart. (Gen.6.5-8; Jer.17.9; Mt.5.27-37)

2. God can create new nature in the heart through Christ. (Eph.4.17; 2 Cor.5.17; Jer. 31.34;, Ps34.4-5;Rev.21.5)

3. Let us always pray for the renewed heart in Christ and live in truth and purity. (Eph.4.24).

   Amen!

SERMON NO.44/A-44

Fifth Sunday After Pentecost

M/EW   *Scripture Readings:*
Ps. 119.89-96   Rom.13.8-14
Gen.50.15-21   Mt.5.38-48

*Theme: Our love for others should be without any limit,
          like the love of God*

Sermon Outline:

1. Joseph practiced godly love. (Gen.50.51-21)

2. Jesus taught to love the enemies. (Mt.5.38-48)

3. Let us practice godly love, which has no limit. (Rom.13.8-
    14; 1 Cor.13.40-8) Amen!

SERMON NO.45/A-45

Sixth Sunday After Pentecost

M/EW   *Scripture Readings:*
                    Ps. 119.9-16   Jas.1.22-27
                    Jer.7.1-15   Mt.7.21-29

Theme: Be doers, not merely hearers of the Word

Sermon Outline:

1. Those who believe and obey the Word of God are
    blessed and saved by God. (Mt.7.21-23)

2. Doing the Word of God is like house on the rock.
    (Mt.7.24-25)

3. Doing the Word of God is true worship. (Jer.7.1-15;
    Rom.12.1)

4. Doing the Word of God is to practice true religions.
    (Jas.1.22-27)

5. The doers of the Word of God shall enter into the
    kingdom of God. (Mt.7.21) Amen!

SERMON NO.46/ A-46

Seventh Sunday After Pentecost

M/EW   *Scripture Readings:*
                    Ps. 99   1 Cor.9.13-23
                    Num.27.15-23   Mt.9.35-10.16

Theme: **God himself commissions those who do his work**

Sermon Outline:

1. God appoints his servants. (Num.27.15-23)

2. Jesus appointed his disciples to be his witnesses. (Mt.9.35-10.16)

3. God's servants must do their work with strong determination and faithfulness. (1.Cor.9.13-23) Amen!

SERMON NO.47/A-47

Eighth Sunday After Pentecost

M/EW　　　　*Scripture Readings:*

Ps.56　　　　　　　Phil. 1.27-30

Is. 41.8-13　　　　　Mt. 10.24-33

Theme: *Jesus teaches to be bold in God's service*

Sermon Outline:

1. Persecution and sufferings are bound to come in God's mission in the world. (Phil. 1.27-30; Mt. 10.16-21)

2. God gives them boldness, protection and showers his blessings upon the faithful servants and on their work. (Ps.56; Is 41.8-13; Mt.10.24-33; Acts 4.31)

3. Jesus taught his disciples not to fear, and assured them of his timely help and rewards. (Mt.5.10-12; 10.24-33).

   Amen!

SERMON NO.48/A-48

Ninth Sunday After Pentecost

M/ EW　　　　*Scripture Readings:*

Ps. 106　　　　　　Rom.10.13-21

Ex.32.1-14　　　　Mt.11.16-24

Theme: ***The messengers of God are often unheeded***

Sermon Outline:

1. The unbelieving and unrighteous servants deserve judgment and sufferings. (Ex.32.1-14; Mt.11.16-24)

2. Those who hear the Gospel and call upon the Lord are saved. (Rom. 10.13-15)

3. Let us obey the voice of the Lord, and be saved by his grace. (Rom. 10.13; Eph.2;8) Amen!

SERMON NO.49/A-49

Tenth Sunday After Pentecost

M/EW   *Scripture Readings:*

Ps. 121   Heb.4.14-5.5

Ex.19.1-8   Mt. 11.25-30

Theme: ***God cares for those who are heavily burdened***

Sermon Outline:

1. God saved the Israelites from the Egyptian bondage. (Ex.19.1-6)

2. Jesus invites all those who are heavy laden, so that he might give them peace and rest. (Mt.11.25-30)

3. Let us trust in the Lord, because he always takes care of his people, the poor and the righteous. (Ps.121).

    Amen!

SERMON NO.50/A-50

Eleventh Sunday After Pentecost

M/EW   *Scripture Readings:*

Ps. 141.1-9   Jas. 3.1-12

Jer.23.23-32   Mt.12.31-37

Theme: ***We are judged by our words, which reveal what is in our heart***

Sermon Outline:

1. Our words reveal our heart. (Mt.12.33-35)

2. Sin against the Holy Spirit is not forgiven. (Mt. 12.31-32)

3. We must be watchful of what we speak, as it is compared to fire. (Jas. 3.1-12)

4. Let us resolve to speak the truth in love. (Eph. 4.16) Amen!

SERMON NO.51/A-51

Twelfth Sunday After Pentecost

M/EW   *Scripture Readings:*
              Ps. 93   1 Jn.2.28-3.3
              Ex. 34.29-35   Lk.9.28-36

Theme: **The transfiguration of Christ confirms his Divinity**

Sermon Outline:

1. Moses' complexion was enlightened during his 40 days with God on Mount Sinai. (Ex.34.29-35)

2. Jesus' complexion and garments were brightened in his transfiguration. (Lk.9.28-36)

3. During his transfiguration it was declared from heaven that Jesus is the Son of God. (Lk.9.35)

4. It was also declared that the world should listen to Jesus. (Lk.9.35)

5. Let us rejoice that we shall be like the glorified Jesus (1 Jn. 3.2-3) Amen!

SERMON NO.52/A-52

Thirteenth Sunday After Pentecost

M /EW   *Scripture Readings:*
              Ps. 119. 65-72   Phil. 3.4b-11
              Gen. 12.1-7   Mt. 13.44-52

Theme: No sacrifice is too great for those who seek the kingdom of God (Gen 12.1-7)

Sermon Outline:

1. Abraham obeyed God for the sake of His Kingdom. (Gen. 12.1-7)

2. The kingdom of God is precious and holy, where there is no place of evil. (Mt.13.44-52)

3. The kingdom of God was very costly for St. Paul. (Phil.3.4-11)

4. Let us seek his kingdom and righteousness. (Mt.6.33) Amen!

SERMON NO.53/A-53

Fourteenth Sunday After Pentecost

M/EW   *Scripture Readings:*
                Ps. 145   Acts 14.8-18
                Gen.41.49-42.5   Mt.14.13-21

Theme: God provides food for the hungry

Sermon Outline:

1. By the wisdom of God Joseph supplied food to the hungry world. (Gen.41.49-42.5)

2. By the power of God Jesus provided food to the five thousand. (Mt.14.13-21)

3. God demonstrated His wonder working power in the ministry of St. Paul. (Acts 14.8-18)

4. Let us praise God for His wonderful deeds and gracious provisions for his people. (Ps.145; Phil.4.19)

    Amen!

SERMON NO.54/A-54

Fifteenth Sunday After Pentecost

M/EW   *Scripture Readings:*

Ps.107.1-3; 23-32   Jas.1.2-8

1 King 19.1-13   Mt. 14.23-33

Theme: In the storms of life the Lord is near at hand to save

Sermon Outline:

1. God saved Elijah from his enemy and hunger. (1Kings 19.1-13a)

2. Jesus saved Peter from sinking in the sea. (Mt. 14.23-33)

3. The Psalmist reminds the redeemed to give thanks to the wonder working Saviour. (Ps.107)

4. Let us rejoice and praise God for His saving hands in times of trials. (Jas.1.2-8). Amen

SERMON NO.55/A-55

Sixteenth Sunday After Pentecost

M/EW   *Scripture Readings:*

Ps.4   Heb. 11.1-10

Gen, 32.22-30   Mt.15.21-28

Theme: The rewards of persevering in faith

Sermon Outline:

1. Jacob wrestled with the angel and prevailed, and was rewarded with the great name, Israel. (Gen.32-22-30)

2. The Gentile woman prayed to Jesus for healing her daughter, and she was healed. (Mt.15.21-28)

3. If we persevere in our faith, the Lord is faithful to reward. (Ps.4; Heb.11; Rom.1.17) Amen!

SERMON NO.56/A-56

Seventeenth Sunday After Pentecost

M/EW   *Scripture Readings:*

Ps. 120   1 Cor.4.7-14

Is. 53. 1-4, 10-11   Mt. 16.13-24

Theme: The way of the Cross

Sermon Outline:

1   The path of God's servants are full of shame and sorrow. (Is.53)

2.   The way of the Cross is full of sufferings and shame. (Mt.16.13-24)

3.   St. Paul taught that the way of the Cross is a way of humility. (1 Cor.4.7-11)

4.   The way of the cross must end with the heavenly glory through Christ. (1 Cor.1.18; 2 Tim.2.11) Amen!

SERMON NO.57/A-57

Eighteenth Sunday After Pentecost

M/ EW   *Scripture Readings:*

Ps. 25   1 Cor.8

Deut.13.1-5   Mt.18.7-14

Theme: Though we have to face temptations, it is God's will that all should be saved

Sermon Outline:

1.   God is One, and there is no other. (1 Cor.8.4-6)

2.   People with weak faith fall into temptations. (Deut.13.1-5; 1 Cor.8.7-9)

3.   People with strong faith must help the weak. (1Cor.8.10-13)

4.   Let us overcome temptations and be saved by God's grace. (Jn.16.33; Rev.3.19-22)   Amen!

SERMON NO. 58/A-58

Nineteenth Sunday After Pentecost

M/EW   *Scripture Readings:*
              Ps.86   2 Cor. 1.23-2.11
              Is.45.1-15   Mt.18.21-33

Theme: Those who refuse to forgive cannot be forgiven

Sermon Outline:

1. Jesus' teachings on forgiveness. (Mt.18.21-22; 5.23-26)
2. Those who forgive shall be forgiven. (Mt.18.23-35; 2 Cor.2.10a)
3. God forgives those who call on him in Prayer. (Ps.86.5)
4. Let us forgive one another, so that we may be forgiven. (Mt.6.12)

   Amen!

SERMON NO. 59/A-59

Twentieth Sunday After Pentecost

M/EW   *Scripture Readings:*
              Ps.16   Rom.5.6-11
              Deut.7.6-8   Mt.20.1-16

Theme: God gives us far more than we deserve

Sermon Outline:

1. Jesus' parable of the generous householder. (Mt.20.1-16)
2. Jesus graciously gave his life to save sinners. (Rom.5.6-11; 6.23; Eph.2.8)
3. Let us praise God for His free gift of eternal life through Christ. (Ps 16.10; Rom.5.1-2; 6.23) Amen!

SERMON NO.60/A-60

Twenty- first Sunday After Pentecost

M/E   *Scripture Readings:*
                Ps.81   Heb. 12.18-29
                Prov.9.1-6   Mt.22.1-14

Theme: *God's gracious invitation calls for a glad and willing response*

Sermon Outline:

1   Jesus' parable of the wedding feast. (Mt.22.1-14)

2. God looks for people who are worthy and willing to be his guest. (Mt.22.7-14)

3. The wedding feast resembles the Kingdom of Heaven. (Rev.3.19-22)

4. Let us thank God for his open invitation to heaven. (Heb.12.28) Amen!

SERMON NO.61/A-61

Twenty–second Sunday After Pentecost

M/EW   *Scripture Readings*
                Ps. 119.97-104   Gal.5.2-15
                Deut.10.12-19   Mt.22.34-40

Theme: Love sums up and fulfils every Law

Sermon Outline:

1. Jesus' new commandments are based on Love. (Mt.22.34-40; Mk.12.31)

2. The whole law is summed up in one word, Love. (Gal.5.14

3. Let us obey the Law and practice Love. Amen!

SERMON NO.62/A-62

Twenty –third Sunday After Pentecost

M/EW　　　　　*Scripture Readings:*

Ps.62   Rom.2.17-24

Jer.5.1-5,30-31   Mt.23.1-12

Theme:　Preaching is useless, if it is contradicted by the way we live

Sermon Outline:

1. The Israelites failed to walk in the ways of the Lord including their priest and prophets. (Jer.5)

2. The Pharisees failed to practice what they preached. (Mt.23.3)

3. The preacher should live in accordance to what they preach. (Rom.2.17-24; Mt.5.1-26)

4. Let us pray for the preachers, so that they might live what they preach. Amen!

SERMON NO.63/A-63

Twenty- fourth Sunday After Pentecost

M/EW　　　　　*Scripture Readings:*

Ps.26   1 Cor.3.10-17

Gen. 39.1-6a   Mt.25.14-30

Theme:　God will call us to account for our stewardship of time and talents

Sermon Outline:

1　Joseph was an ideal steward in Egypt. (Gen.39)

2. Jesus' parable of the talents. (Mt.25.14-30)

3. God is pleased with the faithful and productive stewards. (Mt.25.21)

4. The unfaithful and wicked stewards shall be punished. (Mt.25.30)

5. Let us always remain prepared to give an account to the Lord of the Days of judgment, which is coming soon. (Mt.3.2) Amen !

SERMON NO.64/A-64

Twenty –fifth Sunday After Pentecost

M /EW   *Scripture Readings*
Ps.87   Rom.9.30-10
Ruth 1.6-22   Mt. 21.23-32

Theme: Despised outsiders are often more open to God's call than those despise them

Sermon Outline:

1. The Gentile widow accompanied her mother-in-law. (Ruth1.6-22)

2. A repentant sinner shall enter into heaven than an Israelite. (Mt.21.28-32)

3. St. Paul argues for the Gentile believers. (Rom.9-10)

4. Let us come to the Lord with humility and repentance than despising others. (Ps. 51.17; 1 Pet.5.6-7) Amen !

SERMON NO.65/A-65

Twenty-sixth Sunday After Pentecost

M/EW   *Scripture Readings:*
Ps .79   Rom.8.18=25
Job.2.1-10   Mt.24.1-14

Theme: Christian cannot expect to be shield from all trials

Sermon Outline:

1. The righteous Job was allowed by God to be tried by Satan. (Job.2.1-10)

2. The whole world is in trials due to man's multiple sins. (Mt.24.1-14; Rom.8.22-23)

3. Let us trust in the triumphant Lord Jesus, who is able to help us overcome trials and temptations mercifully. (Jn. 16.33; 2 Cor.5.21; Heb.2.17-18)   Amen!

SERMON NO.66/A-66

Twenty –seventh and Last Sunday After Pentecost

M/EW   *Scripture Readings:*
          Ps.98   1 Jn.3.16-27
          Ezek.34.17-24   Mt.25.31-46

Theme: We must all appear before the judgment seat of Christ

Sermon Outline:

1. At the Day of judgment, the Lord shall separate the righteous from the sinners. (Ezek34.17-24; Mt.25.31-46)

2. The sinners shall be punished and the righteous shall be saved eternally in heaven. (Mt.25.46; Ps.1.5-6)

3. The forgiven shall be rewarded in heaven and the cursed shall perish in the hell-fire for ever and ever. (Am.5.18-21;Jn 3.16-21)

4. Let us prepare to appear before the throne of grace thankfully and joyfully on the Day of Judgment. Amen!

CHAPTER TWO

Sermon Outlines
for YEAR B (67-129)

SERMON NO.67/B-1

Fourth Sunday Before Christmas

(Advent I)

M/EW   *Scripture Readings:*

Ps.80   1 Thess.5.1-11

Is.64.1-8   Mk. 13.24-37

Theme: Watchful expectation for the appearing of Christ

Sermon Outline:

1. Christ was expected to come as the great and wonder working creator. (Is.64.1-4)

2. Christ was expected to come as the God of the living. (Mk.13.26-27; 1 Thess. 5.1-11)

3. Christ was expected to come as the God of love. (Mk.13.28-34)

4. Christ was expected to come as the Son of David. (Mk.13.35-37)

5. Let us wait upon the Lord, who is coming again in heavenly glory and honour. (Acts 1.11; Col.3.1-4; Phili.1.9-11) Amen!

SERMON NO.68/B-2

Third Sunday Before Christmas

(Advent II)

M/EW   *Scripture Readings:*
                Ps.119. 129-144   2 Tim.3.14-45
                Zech.1.1-6   Jn.5.31-47

Theme: *The Word of God demands response from its hearers*

Sermon Outline:

1. The Word of God is wonderful, which gives light to the readers. (Ps.119.129-144)

2. The Word of God proclaims that the Day of the Lord shall be the Day of the last judgment. (Jn.5.31-47; 2 Tim.3.14-17)

3. Let us urgently proclaim the message of the Lord's second coming. (2 Tim.4.1-5) Amen!

SERMON NO.69/B-3

Second Sunday Before Christmas

(Advent III)

M/EW   *Scripture Readings:*
                Ps.146   Jas.5.1-9
                Mal.3.1-7   Mt.11.2-11

Theme: *The coming of Christ is good news for the oppressed*

Sermon Outline:

1. The Lord is coming soon as the refiner's fire. (Mal.3.1-7)

2. He came to heal the sick, caste out demons, and to proclaim goods news for the poor and the righteous. (Mt.11.2-11; Jas.5.7-7)

3. He came to save the people under exploitation by the riches. (Jas.5.1-9)

4. Let us praise God and trust in Him, who is the God of love and righteousness. (Ps.146)
    Amen!

SERMON NO.70/B-4

Second Sunday Before Christmas

(Advent IV)

M/EW   *Scripture Readings:*
                Ps. 89.19-37   Phil.4.4-7
                Zech. 2.10-13   Lk.1.26-38

Theme: The Lord's coming gives joy and peace to his people

Sermon Outline:

1. The Lord has fulfilled his promise to come and live amidst his people. (Zech.2.11)

2. In the fullness of time angel Gabriel declared the Lord's coming into the world in the line of David. (Lk.1.26-38; Gal. 4.4-7; Ps.89.19-37)

3. Let us praise God for the availability of joy and peace in Christ. (Phil.4.4-7; Jn.10.10)

    Amen !

SERMON NO.71/B-5

The Christmas Day

M/EW   *Scripture Readings:*
                Ps.76   Heb.1.1-12
                Is.9.2-7   Jn.1.1-14

Theme: The birth of the saviour who is word made flesh

Sermon Outline:

1. The Son of God and the prince of Peace has come into the world. (Is.9.2-7; Heb.1.1-12)

2. The Lord is the Word made flesh, who was the creator of all things. (Jn.1.1-14)

3   The Lord is the light of the world, and his followers shall not walk in darkness. (Jn.1.4-5; 8.12; Mt.5.14-16)

4. Let us sing new songs and exult the Lord, who is the King of Kings and the Lord of Lords. (Ps.56) Amen !

SERMON NO.72/B-6

First Sunday After Christmas

M/EW   *Scripture Readings:*
              Ps.148   Acts 3.1-16
              Ex.3.13-17   Lk.2.15-21

Theme: *The Name of Jesus*

Sermon Outline:

1. The Lord God introduced himself to Moses, as the God of Israel. (Ex.3.13-17; Dan.5.6)

2. The Lord is Holy and Righteous. (Acts. 3.14)

3. The name Jesus was given by the angel of God. (Lk.2.21, Mt.1.21)

4. Let us praise God for the saving name of Jesus. (Ps.148.5; Acts.4.12) Amen !

SERMON NO.73/B-7

Second Sunday After Christmas

M /EW   *Scripture Readings:*
              Ps.34.11-22   Gal.41-7
              Prov.8.1,22-31   Jn.1.9-18

Theme: *We are sharers in the Sonship of Christ*

Sermon Outline:

1. Jesus Christ is the Son of God. (Jn. 1.14,18)

2. Jesus' followers share His Divine Sonship. (Gal.4.1-7)

3. Jesus Christ, as the Word made flesh reflects and demonstrates the wisdom of God . (Prov.8.22-31; Jn.1.14)

4. Let us praise God at all times. (Ps.34.1) Amen!

SERMON NO.74/B-8

Third Sunday After Christmas

(Baptism of Jesus)

M/EW   *Scripture Readings:*
               Ps.72   1 Jn. 5.5-11
               Is.42.1-7   Mk.1.4-11

Theme: At his baptism Jesus is revealed as the Son of God

Sermon Outline:

1. Jesus was baptized by John the Baptist in a new ritual founded by himself. (Mk.1.4-11)

2. At his baptism it was declared that he is the Son of God. (Mk.1.11)

3. At his baptism the Holy Spirit descended upon him and confirmed as the anointed and the promised Messiah. (Mk.1.10: Is.42.1-7)

4. Let us praise God for giving His Son for our salvation Amen!

SERMON NO.75/B-9

Fourth Sunday After Christmas

M/EW   *Scripture Readings:*
               Ps.17   Phil.1.19-29
               Ex.33.12-17   Jn.1.35-42

Theme: *True followers of Christ seek to live always in his presence*

Sermon Outline:

1. God promised to send His presence with Moses. (Ex.33.12-17)

2. Jesus lives with his disciples. (Jn. 1.35-42; Mt. 1.23; 28.20)

3. Jesus' disciples are expected be with him in all circumstances. (Phil.1.19-29; 2 Tim.2.11-13)

4. Let us strive to behold the face of the Lord at all times like David. (Ps. 17.15; 23.6; 73.28; 84.10)

SERMON NO.76/B-10

Fifth Sunday After Christmas
(Leprosy Sunday)

M/EW   *Scripture Readings:*
                     Ps. 123   Acts.5.12-16
                     2 Kings 5.1-14   Mk.1.40-45
                                                  or
                                                  Lk.17.11-19

Theme: *God suffers with all those who suffer in this world*

Sermon Outline:

1   God healed Naaman, the leper. (2 Kings 5.1-27)

2. Jesus touched and healed the leper. (Mk.1.40-45)

3. Disciples of Christ healed the sick in the name of Jesus. (Acts.5.12-16)

4. The faithful witness of the slave girl of Naaman and the unfaithfulness and greed of Gehazi. (2Kings 5)

5. Let us be kind to the sick and the needy people, and make efforts and prayer for their well-being.

    Amen!

SERMON NO.77/B-11

Sixth Sunday After Christmas

M/EW   *Scripture Readings:*

Ps.71   Gal.1.11-24

Jer.1.4-10   Lk.5.1-11

*Theme: Those whom God calls to his service are equipped
for their work*

Sermon Outline:

1. Jesus preached at the sea shores. (Lk.5.1-3)

2. Jesus knew the problem of Peter, and helped him
to catch a great number of fish miraculously. (Lk.5.
4-7)

3. Peter and his partners realized the greatness of Jesus.
(Lk.5.8-10)

4. Jesus, called him to make fishers of men. (Lk.5.10-11;
Jer 1.4-10); Gal .1.11-24)

5. Let us believe in Christ and proclaim his good news to
the world around us. (1 Cor. 9.16) Amen !

SERMON NO. 78/B-12

Ninth Sunday Before Easter

M/EW   *Scripture Readings:*

Ps.65   Acts 17.22-31

Gen.9.8-16   Mt.6.25-31

*Theme: The World is full of signs which point to the goodness
and providence of God*

Sermon Outline:

1. God's covenant sign with Noah and his descendents.
(Gen .9.8-16; Mt.6.25-31)

2. The worship of the unknown God is a sign of his existence. (Acts.17.22-31)

3. We must praise God for his wonderful deeds in nature, and the work for our salvation. (Ps.65). Amen !

SERMON NO.79/B-13

Eighth Sunday Before Easter

M/EW   *Scripture Readings:*

Ps. 55   Eph.2.14-18

Judg.9.1-6   Mt.26.27-56

Theme: ***Strife and violence are result of human sinfulness, from which Christ came to save***

Sermon Outline:

1. The evils of Abimelech brought curse upon the people of Shechem. (Judg.9.1-6; Esth.7.9-10)

2. Judah's plot of betrayal brought curse upon himself {Mt.26.47-56; Acts.1.16 20)

3. But Jesus brought salvation to the world through his redeeming death and purifying blood. (Eph.2.14-18)

4. Let us trust in the Lord and practice righteousness (Ps.55.23) Amen!

SERMON NO.80/B-14

Seventh Sunday Before Easter

M/EW   *Scripture Readings:*

Ps. 30   1 Tim. 1.12-17

Is.57.15-21   Mk.2.13-17

Theme: ***God has sent His Son to give us healing both in body and soul***

Sermon Outline:

1. God has resolved to save the humble people. (Is.57.15-21)

2. Jesus forgave the sin of the paralytic and healed him. (Mk.2.1-12)

3. God forgives the sins of the humble and contrite repentant. (Mk.2.13-17; 1 Tim.1.12-17)

4. Let us humble ourselves like St. Paul and be healed both in body and soul by the grace of our Lord and saviour. Amen!

SERMON NO.81/B-15

Ash Wednesday

M/EW   *Scripture Readings:*
                Ps. 130   2 Cor.5.17-6.2
                Joel 2.12-17   Lk.13.1-9

Theme: God calls everyone urgently to repent

Sermon Outline:

1. Joel is urging people to repent to be forgiven by God. (Joel 2.12-17)

2. God calls everyone and gives ample opportunities to repent and to be renewed and reconciled to God through Christ. (Lk.13.1-9; 2 Cor.5.17-21)

3. The Lord entrust his servants to be his ambassadors for this urgent ministry of reconciliation, as the Day of the Lord is near, as to-day. (2 Cor.5.17-6.2)

4. Let us respond to Lord's call and become his ambassadors, so that many may repent and be saved through Christ. Amen!

SERMON NO.82/B-16

Sixth Sunday Before Easter

(Lent I)

M/EW   *Scripture Readings:*
               Ps.143.1-11   Jas.1.12-18
               Gen.3.1-9   Mk. 1.9-13
                                       or Mt.4.1-11

Theme: **The contrast between the failure of Adam and the obedience of Jesus, whose victory we are called to share**

Sermon Outline:

1. Adam and Eve failed to obey God. (Gen.3.1-19)

2. The humble obedience and victory of Jesus. (Mk.1.9-13; Phil.2.8-11)

3. Jesus' followers are called to share his victory as the first fruit in the whole creation. (Jas.1.12-18; Cor.15.23)

4. Let us rejoice for the humble obedience and victory of our Lord Jesus Christ and share his victory and glory thankfully. (Jn.16.33; 1 Cor.15.51-58).   Amen!

SERMON NO.83/B-17

Fifth Sunday Before Easter

(Lent II)

M/EW   *Scripture Readings:*
               Ps. 109.1-5,21-31   2 Cor.11.21b-31
               Ex.3,1-12   *or*
               Mk.8.27-35   Heb.11.23-27

Theme: **Jesus the Messiah accepted suffering according to his Father's will, and calls his disciples to follow him**

Sermon Outline:

1. The Jews suffered in Egypt at the will of God (Ex.3.1-12; Gen 15.13)

2. Jesus prophesied his own suffering at the will of the Father. (Mk.8.27-35; Mt.26.52-56)

3. Jesus calls his disciples to remain prepared to suffer for His sake. (Mk.34-35; Mt.5.10-12)

4. St. Paul suffered for the sake of Christ and his Gospel. (2 Cor.11.11.21-13)

5. Those who suffer and die for the sake of the Lord and His kingdom shall also live with Him eternally. (Tim.2.11-12;1 Pet.5.-11; Rev.3.19-22) Amen !

SERMON NO.84/B-18

Fourth Sunday Before Easter

(Lent III)

M/EW   *Scripture Readings:*
Ps.97   2 Pet.1.13-19
Ex.34.29-35   Mk.9.2-10

Theme: Transfiguration reveals the true glory and authority of Jesus, the Son of God

Sermon Outline:

1. Moses' face was shining as he remained near God. (Ex.34.29-35; Ps.97;11)

2. Jesus' face was brightened due to his heavenly fellowship during His transfiguration. (Mk.9.4)

3. During His transfiguration Jesus was declared as the beloved Son of God. (Mk.9.7)

4. Let us pray to God to be near Him as desired by the disciples of Christ. (Mk.9.5;Heb.4.10;10.22; Jas.4.8; Ps.23.6) Amen !

SERMON NO.85/B-19

Third Sunday Before Easter

(Lent IV)

M/EW   *Scripture Readings:*

Ps.123   1 Cor .4.6-21

Num.12.1-8   Mk. 10.35-45

Theme: ***True greatness is shown in humble service and self-sacrifice***

Sermon Outline:

1. Miriam and Aaron grumbled against Moses. (Num.12.1-8)

2. James and John were greedy for higher positions. (Mk 10.35-42)

3. Moses and Jesus were great as humble obedient servants of God. (Num. 12.3; Mk.10.45; Jn.1.29; Phil. 2.5-11; Rev.7.14)

4. As the followers of Jesus, we must be humble, and ready to sacrifice all things for Christ and for His kingdom. (1 Pet.6.6-11; Phil.3.7-21; 1 Cor.4.6-21) Amen!

SERMON NO.86/B-20

Second Sunday Before Easter

(Lent V)

M/EW   *Scripture Readings:*

Ps. 31.1-16   1 Cor. 1.18-25

Is. 44.24-28   Mk.12.1-12

Theme: ***The wisdom and power of God are most clearly revealed in the weakness and foolishness of the Cross.***

Sermon Outline:

1. The parable of the wicked tenants, who killed their Master's son, which indicates Jesus' crucification. (Mk.12.1-8; 8.31-33)

2. The rejected stone became the cornerstone a marvellous simile of Jesus authentic Messiahship. (Mk.12.9-12; Ps.118.22-23; 1 Pet.2.7-8)

3. God anointed a Gentile king to redeem Israel – a peculiar Divine action by the Supreme Almighty. (Is.44.24-28; Rom.11.33-36)

4. Jesus, the crucified Saviour, although like a broken vessel, wonderfully becomes the source of the living water for the thirsty world in God's providence. (Ps.31.12; Jn.4.41;Is.55.1)

5. The weakness and foolishness of the Cross reveals the wisdom and power of God to save the perishing world. (1 Cor.1.18-25)

6. Let us humbly trust in the Lord and proclaim the Christ crucified. (1 Cor.1.18, 30-31) Amen!

SERMON NO.87/B-21

Sunday Before Easter –Palm Sunday

(Lent VI in the Passion Week)

M/EW   *Scripture Readings:*
                   Ps.89.34-51   Heb.5.1-10
                   Is.52.13-5.3.12   Mk.14. 1-15.47
                                            or
                                            15.1-39

Theme: Christ enters Jerusalem to offer his life for the salvation of the world

Sermon Outline:

1. The Master of Passover was prepared to be the Passover Lamb. (Mk.14.12;12.1-27)

2. The king on the back of the ass became the saviour of the world. (Mk.14.11-15; Is 52-53; Jn.3.14-36)

3. The eternal high priest, in the order of Melchizedek, was humbly judged by the wicked Jews and worldly kings. (Heb.5.10; 7.25; Is.9.6-7; Mk.14-15)

4. Let us praise God for the humble king, who was humiliated and died, so that we might receive heavenly glory and eternal life.

   Amen!

SERMON NO.88/B-22

Monday Before Easter

(Passion Week)

M/EW   *Scripture Readings:*
            Ps. 27.2-5. 13-14   Lk.19.41-48
            Is.42.1-7

Theme: Jesus' cleansing the Jerusalem Temple

Sermon Outline:

1. Jesus foresaw the Jews' further persecution by foreign rulers due to their sins and unbelief over his Messiahship. (Lk.1.68-75; 19.41-44;Is.42)

2. Jesus rebuked the traders in the Temple premises, as it should be the house of prayers. (Lk.19.45-46)

3. The Jewish leaders sought to kill Jesus. (Lk.19.47-48)

4. Let us believe in the Messiahship of Jesus and worship and obey him faithfully. Amen!

SERMON NO.89/B-23

Tuesday Before Easter

(Passion Week)

M/EW   *Scripture Readings:*
                Ps. 71.1-2,9-12   Mk.14.1-9
                Is.49.1-7

Theme: Jesus' anointing before death

Sermon Outline:

1. Jesus in the house of Simon the leper at Bethany. (Mk.14.1-9)

2. A woman anointing the Lord with costly oil. (Mk.14.3)

3. Ungodly view of the worldly people. (Mk 14.4-9)

4. In spite of humiliation and sufferings the Lord brings blessings, and is glorified in fulfillment of the scriptures. (Is.49.1-7; Phil. 2.5-11)

5. Let us praise God for Christ our Lord and saviour, and rededicate ourselves at his feet to receive multiple blessings. Amen !

SERMON NO.90/B-24

Wednesday Before Easter
(Passion Week)

M/EW   *Scripture Readings:*
                Ps.55.12-14, 20-22
                Is.50.4-10   Lk.22.1-6

Theme: *Judah's conspiracy with the Jewish leaders to betray Jesus Christ*

Sermon Outline:

1. The conspiracy to betray Jesus at a lonely place. (Lk.22.1-6; Ps.55)

2. God allowed Jesus to be betrayed and to die for the world as a suffering servant the Messiah, according to His divine plan. (Is.50.4-10)

3. Let us meditate upon the sufferings and death of Jesus for our sake, and resolve to proclaim the message of love and salvation to the perishing world. Amen!

SERMON NO. 91/B-25

Maundy Thursday
(The Last Supper)

M/EW   *Scripture Readings:*

Ps. 116.1-2, 12-19   1 Cor.11.23-29

Ex.12.1-8, 11-14   Jn.13.1-7, 34-35

or   *or*

Jer.31.31-34   6.35-39,47-51

*Theme: **Jesus gives his disciples a new commandment and institutes the Lord's Supper***

Sermon Outline:

1. Jesus is the final Passover Lamb. (Ex.12.1-8; Heb 9.11-28; Jn.1.29; Rev.7.14)

2. Jesus' last Passover Feast was His Last Supper. (Jn.13.1-17; 1Cor.11.23-29)

3. At His Last Supper, Jesus opens the promised new covenant, and gave the new commandment. (Jer.31.31-34; 1Cor.11.23-29)

4. Jesus' Last Supper initiates man's union with the Holy God through his sacrificial death. (Jn.35-51; 1Cor.10.16-22; Eph.1.4-10)

5. The Lord's supper reflects our witness to his death for our eternal life. (1Cor.11.26)

6. Let us celebrate the Lord's Supper in its true meaning, and proclaim his death and resurrection. Amen!

SERMON NO.92/B-26

The Good Friday

M/EW   *Scripture Readings:*
                Ps.69   Heb.10.4-24
                Gen.22.1-18   Jn.18.1-19.42

Theme: The victory of the Cross

Sermon Outline:

1. Abraham's preparedness to sacrifice his only son was a victory of his faith. (Gen.22.1-18)

2. Jesus' self-offering on the Cross as a Lamb of God once for all the Divine plan of God stands for his victory as the promised Messiah and the saviour Lord. (Jn. 1.29;11.50;19.11,24.28; Mt.26.54; Heb.10.12;etc)

3. Jesus' victory on the cross was rewarded by the Father to sit at His right hand in Heaven. (Heb.1.3-4; 10.12)

4. Let us praise God for His gracious Divine plan for our salvation the cost of His Son Jesus' offering on the Cross. (1 Cor.1.18) Amen!

SERMON NO.93/B-27

Easter Sunday

M/EW   *Scripture Readings:*
                Ps 118   Col.3.1-4
                Ex.15.1-2,9-21   Jn.20.1-18
                                             or
                                             Lk.24.13-35

Theme: *The risen, He is risen, indeed. Alleluia!*

Sermon Outline:

1. The Exodus events reflect the Almighty power of God in nature. (Ex.15;Jos.3-6)

2. The Easter event reflects the power of God over death by raising Jesus from among the dead. (Jn.20;Lk.24)

3. The resurrection of Jesus has many eyewitnesses, as narrated in the Scriptures. (Jn.20-21;Lk.24; Mt.28;Mk.16)

4. The resurrection of Jesus assures the resurrection of His believers and followers. (1Cor.15.12-58)

5. The resurrection of our Lord also challenges Christians' moral elevation through the development of higher and heavenly qualities, and be highly rewarded. (Col.3.-4)

6. Let us praise God and say, 'Alleluia," for the risen Lord brings multiple blessings Amen!

SERMON NO.94/B-28

First Sunday After Easter

M/EW   Scripture Readings:
              Ps.111   1 Jn.1.1-7
              Acts 4.32-35   Jn.20.19-31

Theme: *Joy and peace, power and new life are given through the resurrection of Christ*

Sermon Outline:

1. The visions of the risen Lord brought joy and peace among the disciples of Christ. (Jn. 20.9-31)

2. Jesus' resurrection brought joy and peace, power and new life among his believers. (Acts 4.32-35; 1 Jn.1.1-7)

3. Let us praise God for the risen Lord and proclaim this glorious message to the world. Amen!

SERMON NO.95/B-29

Second Sunday After Easter

M/ EW   *Scripture Readings:*
                 Ps. 57   1 Jn.2.18-25
                 Acts 5.27-42   Lk.24.36-48

Theme: *Witness to Christ's resurrections*

Sermon Outline:

1. Jesus frequently visited his disciples soon after his resurrection, and confirmed it. (Lk.24. Mt.28. Mk.16, Jn. 20-21)

2. Jesus' resurrection brings fulfillment of the scriptures that he is the Christ. (Lk.24.47; Hos.6.2; Ps.16.16; Is. 25.8; 1 Jn.2.22; etc)

3. The resurrection of Jesus strengthened faith in his Messiahship and supported the establishment of the early church inspite of persecution and doubts. (Acts.5.27-42)

4. Let us believe and trust in the risen Lord in all things, and be his witnesses. Amen!

SERMON NO.96/B-30

Third Sunday After Easter

M/EW   *Scripture Readings:*
                 Ps. 113   1 Jn.1.8-2.6
                 Acts.8.14-25   Jn.10.11-18

Theme: *The good shepherd*

Sermon Outline:

1. Jesus is the good shepherd, who gave his life for his sheep. (Jn.10.11-18; 1 Jn.2.2)

2. Jesus' sheep should follow him in obedience to him. (1 Jn.1.8-2.6)

3. Jesus, as the good shepherd takes care of his sheep in all matters. (Ps.23;112)

4. Money cannot buy righteousness or the gifts of the Holy Spirit. (Acts.8.14-25)

5. Let us resolve and pray to be a good sheep of the good shepherd. Amen!

SERMON NO 97/B-31

Fourth Sunday After Easter

M/EW   *Scripture Readings:*
              Ps.145   1 Jn. 4.7-16
              Acts .9.22-31   Jn.13.31-35

Theme: **God is love, and we can only know him if we ourselves show love to others.**

Sermon Outline:

1. Jesus' new commandment is to love God and to love one another. (Jn.13.31-35; 15.1-17; Mk.12.29-31)

2. Our love for one another indicates our love and knowledge of God. (1 Jn.4.7-16)

3. St. Paul's dedicated ministry proves that he knows God and the saviour Lord. (Acts 9.22-31)

4. Let us love one another and demonstrate our knowledge of God in practice. Amen!

SERMON NO.98/B-32

Fifth Sunday After Easter

M/EW   *Scripture Readings:*
              Ps.148   1 Jn.3.23-4.4
              Acts. 11.1-8   Jn.14.21-26

Theme: ***Jesus promises that the spirit of truth and love come to dwell in the church***

Sermon Outline:

1. Jesus taught that the mission of God is the mission of love, truth and peace of God. (Jn. 14.21-26; 1 Jn.3.23)

2. St. Peter's vision proves God's love and concern to save people from all class and castes. (Acts.11.1-8;Jn.3.16)

3. Let us pray and strive to fill our churches with the love, truth and peace of our Lord, and glorify his name Amen!

SERMON NO.99/B-33

The Ascension Day

M/EW   *Scripture Readings:*
                Ps.97   Eph.1.15-23
                Acts.1.1-11   Lk.24.44-53

Theme: ***The Son of Man is exalted at the right hand of God***

Sermon Outline:

1. Jesus Christ the Son of Man and Son of God was exalted at the right hand of the Father in Heaven as a reward to his successful mission in the world. (Acts 1.1-11; Eph 1.15-23; Phil.2.8-11 ; Heb.1.3-4)

2. Jesus' exaltation was also a fulfillment of God's Divine plan as mentioned in the scriptures. (Lk.24.44-53; Jn.14.1-6; Ps.97.6)

3. Let us rejoice and praise God for the Lord's ascension, which assures our ascension with him in his second coming.

   Amen!

SERMON NO.100/B-34

Sixth Sunday After Easter

M/EW   *Scripture Readings:*

Ps. 27   1 Jn.2.28-3.3

Acts 7.54-60   Jn.17.11-19

Theme: ***The ascended Lord upholds those who are united to him by faith***

Sermon Outline:

1. St. Stephen had the vision of the risen and exalted Lord Jesus at his martyrdom. (Acts.7.54-60)

2. The faithful and righteous children of God shall be like Jesus, when he comes again to receive them. (Jn.17.4-24; 1 Jn.2.28-3.3)

3. Let us praise God, and continue to strengthen our faith, so that we might grow into salvation to share his heavenly glory. (Ps.27; 1 Pet.2.1-5; Col.3.1-4)

    Amen!

SERMON NO.101/B-35

Sixth Sunday After Easter

M/EW   *Scripture Readings:*

Ps.27   1 Jn.2.28-3.3

Acts.7.54-60   Jn.17.11-19

Theme: ***The ascended Lord upholds those who are united to him by faith***

Sermon Outline:

1. Stephen had the vision of the risen Lord Jesus at his martyrdom. (Acts.7.54-60)

2. The faithful and the righteous children of God shall be like Jesus at his second coming. (Jn.17.11-24; 1Jn.2.28-3.3)

3. Let us praise God and continue to strengthen our faith in the Lord Jesus to avail the multiple blessings in him. (Ps.27)

Amen!

SERMON NO.102/B-36

The Pentecost Sunday

M /EW   *Scripture Readings:*
                   Ps. 68 *or* 139   I Cor. 12.1-13
                   Acts. 2.1-11   Jn.20.19-23

Theme: The gifts of the Holy Spirit

Sermon Outline:

1. The Holy Spirit was showered upon his people according to his promises. (Acts.18;2.1-11; Joel 2.28-29)

2. The Holy Spirit distributes his fruits differently to different persons for the kingdom of God. (Jn.20.19-23; 1 Cor. 12.1-13; Eph.4.1-16)

3. The Holy Spirit searches our hearts and comforts and strengthens us for our well-being and for the mission of God. (Ps.139; 1 Cor.2.10-14; Acts.1.8; Rom.8.26-27)

4. Let us praise God for the gifts of the Holy Spirit, and allow him to dwell in us to bless us and to empower us to work for the Lord's Kingdom. Amen!

SERMON NO.103/B-37

First Sunday After Pentecost
(Trinity Sunday)

M/EW   *Scripture Readings:*
                  Ps.46   Eph.3.14-21
                  Is.6.1-8   Jn.16.5-15

Theme: God is the Holy Trinity

Sermon Outline:

1. Isaiah's vision of conversion and commission indicate the presence of the Trinity God head. (Is.6.1-8)

2. Jesus' earthly life and teaching reveals the Trinity. (Lk.1.24-41; 3.21-22; Jn. 16.5-15; etc)

3. St. Paul writes about the Trinitatarian ministry of God. (Eph.3.14-21)

4. Let us believe in the Holy Trinity and proclaim this biblical doctrine before others. Amen !

SERMON. NO.104/B-38

Second Sunday After Pentecost

M/EW   *Scripture Readings:*
                Ps. 89.5-8   1 Cor.4.4-21
                Deut.5.22-28   Mk.1.21-28

Theme: The unique authority of Christ our Lord

Sermon Outline:

1. The Lord is more powerful than the devouring fire. (Deut.5.22-28)

2. Jesus Christ had authority over the unclean spirit. (Mk.1.21-28)

3. St. Paul demonstrated the power of Christ in his ministry. (1 Cor.4.4-21)

4. The Lord Jesus Christ is authoritative and all powerful. (Mt.28.18)

5. Let us come to the Lord with fear and faithfulness. Amen!

SERMON NO.105/B-39

Third Sunday After Pentecost

M/EW   *Scripture Readings:*
                  Ps.6   Jas.5.13-20
                  Zeph.3.14-19   Mk.2.1-12

Theme: The Church shares in Christ's authority to heal sickness and sin

Sermon Outline:

1. God had promised to redeem his people from all disasters. (Zeph.3.14-19)

2. God' promises came to be true with the Lord Jesus, when he forgave sins and healed the sick. (Mk.2.1-12)

3. Prayer of the righteous can heal sickness and sins. (Jas.5.13-20)

4. Let us pray that all the Churches of Christ and their members share in Christ's authority to bring forgiveness and healing to the people around them. (Ps .6;2 Chr.7.14; Mt.16.16-20; Jas.5.13-20)   Amen!

SERMON NO.106/B-40

Fourth Sunday After Pentecost

M/EW   *Scripture Readings*
                  Ps.15   2 Cor.3.7-18
                  Deut.5.12-15   Mk.2.23-36

Theme: The spiritual freedom which we have in Christ

Sermon Outline:

1. The Old Testament had servanthood covenant. (Deut.5.12-15)

2. Jesus' ministry was need based. (Mk.2.23-3.6)

3. The Sprit of the Lord gives freedom and eternal life to those who are in Christ. (2 Cor. 3.7-18)

4. The Lord looks for true righteousness to give true freedom, eternal life and heaven glory. (Ps.15; 2 Cor.3.18) Amen!

SERMON NO.B/107/B-41

Fifth Sunday After Pentecost

M/EW   *Scripture Readings:*
Ps.65 Or 149   Acts.4.13-22
1 King 19.12-21   Mk.3.7-19a

Theme: ***The authority of Christ's messengers is based on their living contact with him***

Sermon Outline:

1. Elijah was in regular contact with the Lord in joy and sorrows, so God gave him power and protection. (1 Kings 19.12-21, Ps.65)

2. Jesus was always in close contact with the father, hence could demonstrate wonderful works of deliverance. (Mk.3.7-19a)

3. The disciples and apostles of Christ were in close contact with the Christ through the Holy Spirit, so He gave them power and boldness. (Acts. 4.13-22)

4. Let us praise God Almighty, and maintain intimate relationship with Him through the Spirit, and pray for Christ's authority to be wonder working instruments of deliverance for many. Amen!

SERMON NO.108/B-42

Sixth Sunday After Pentecost

M /EW   *Scripture Readings:*
                Ps.3.11-28   Heb.10.25-39
                Jer.18.18-22   Mk.3.19b-30

Theme: **The spiritual peril of denying the truth of God**

Sermon Outline:

1. Jeremiah prayed to God against his enemies. (Jer.18.18-22)

2. Jesus was misunderstood for working by the power of demons. (Mk.3.19b-30)

3. Work against the Holy Spirit is fearful and unforgiven. (Mk .3.28-30; Heb.10.25-39)

4. Let us believe and honour the work of the Holy Spirit and be blessed. Amen !

SERMON NO.109/B-43

Seventh Sunday After Pentecost

M /EW   *Scripture Readings:*
                Ps. 131   1 Cor. 1.26-2.5
                Hag.2.1-9   Mk.4.26-34

Theme: **From very small beginning God produces great results**

Sermon Outline:

1. God wishes to build his houses with all richness and great splendors. (Hag.2.1-9)

2. The kingdom of God must grow miraculously. (Mk.4.26-34)

3. The Church of Christ and his servants must demonstrate the power and the Spirit inspite of small and poor beginnings. (1 Cor.1.26-2.5)

4. Let us pray that the kingdom of God might grow and be established in Spirit and power. Amen!

SERMON NO.110/B-44

Eight Sunday After Pentecost

M/EW   *Scripture Readings:*

Ps.42   Acts.4.28-31

2 Kings 18.28-19.7   Mk.4.35-41

Theme: God upholds us in times of trouble

Sermon Outline:

1. God was with Elijah in his time of trouble. (2Kings 18.28-19.7)

2. Jesus saved his disciple from drowning in the sea. (Mk.4.35-41)

3. The Lord gave his apostles from their enemies, and gave them power and boldness to proclaim the gospel. (Acts.4.35-41)

4. God shall not fail to help those who come to him in righteous thirst. (Ps.42). Amen!

SERMON NO.111/B-45

Ninth Sunday After Pentecost

M/EW   *Scripture Readings:*

Ps.84 *or* 93   1 Jn.2.28-3.3

Ex.24.12-18   Lk.9.28-36

Theme: *Thanksgiving for the transfiguration of Christ, in whose likeness we are being transformed by the Spirit.*

Sermon Outline:

1. Moses was covered with the glory of God on Mt.Sinai. (Ex.24.12-18)

2. Jesus' raiment was dazzling white during his transfiguration. (Lk.9.28-36)

3. It is prophesied that the children of God shall be glorified in the likeness of Christ Jesus in his second coming. (1 Jn.2.28-3.3; Phil.9-11)

4. Let us pray to the Lord to help us in our preparation to grow into the likeness of Christ. Amen!

SERMON NO.112/B-46

Tenth Sunday After Pentecost

M/EW   *Scripture Readings:*
                    Ps.43   Acts.20.7-12
                    Ezek.47.1-12   Mk.5.21-43

Theme: *The life giving power of God*

Sermon Outline:

1. God is the source of the living water. (Ezek.47.1-12; Jn.4.14)

2. Christ Jesus gave life to the daughter of Jairus. (Mk.5.21.43)

3. St.Paul gave life to Eutychus in the power of God in the name of Christ. (Acts.20.7-12)

4. Let us praise God and exult his holy name for his life giving power. Amen!

SERMON NO.113/B-47

Eleventh Sunday After Pentecost

M/EW   *Scripture Readings:*
              Ps. 40.9-17   Acts.17.1-9
              or 81.8-14, 16
              Ezek.33.30-32   Mk.6.1-6a

*Theme: **Varied reception given to God's messengers***

Sermon Outline:

1. The Lord's messengers are welcome by people like love songs. (Ezek.33.30-32)

2. Jesus experienced that a prophet is not honoured in his own place. (Mk.6.1-6)

3. People sent away the apostles out of fear. (Acts.17.1-9; Mk.5.17)

4. Let us welcome the messengers, who bring the saving knowledge of the Lord. Amen!

SERMON NO.114/B-48

Twelfth Sunday After Pentecost

M /EW   *Scripture Readings:*
               Ps.112   2 Cor.9.6-15
               1 Kings. 17.8-16   Jn.6.1-14

*Theme: **God multiplies the gift of the generous giver***

Sermon Outline:

1. God is faithful to the generous giver. (1Kings.17.8-16)

2. God loves the upright and the cheerful giver. (2 Cor.9.6-15; Ps.112)

3. God multiplies and satisfies the needs of many. (Jn.6.1-14)

4. Let us bring thanks offerings to the Lord cheerfully, and receive multiple blessings from him. Amen!

SERMON NO.115/B-49

Thirteenth Sunday After Pentecost

M /EW   *Scripture Readings:*

Ps.105   Heb.3.1-6

Ex. 16.2-15   Jn.6.22-35

Theme: Jesus is the bread of life

Sermon Outline:

1. God provides plenty of food to the Israelites in the wilderness through Moses. (Ex.16.2-15)

2. Jesus came into the world as the bread of life. (Jn.6. 22-35)

3. Let us come to the Lord with confidence and receive eternal life. Amen!

SERMON NO.116/B-50

Fourteenth Sunday After Pentecost

M/EW   *Scripture Readings:*

Ps.116   Rom.6.1-11

Is.55.1-7   Jn.6.57-57

Theme: Baptism and the Lord's Supper

Sermon Outline:

1. God's new covenant was fulfilled with Christ. (Is.55.1-7 ; Jer.31.31-34; Jn.1.1-18)

2. Baptism opens up entry into the new covenant and new life in Christ. (Rom.6)

3. The Lord's Supper with the body and blood of Christ is the participation in the Divine spiritual

fellowship with the Lord and his people. (Jn.6. 47-57)

4. Let us observe the sacraments of baptism and the Lord's Supper confidently, and celebrate His steadfast love for us. Amen!

SERMON NO.117/B-51

Fifteenth Sunday After Pentecost

M /EW   *Scripture Readings:*

Ps.9   Rom.2.1-11

Is.51   Jn.8.2-11

Theme: God's judgment is just and merciful

Sermon Outline:

1. God is a righteous Judge. (Ps.9)

2. God's judgment shall be just and impartial. (Rom.2. 1-11; Is.51.1-8)

3. Jesus judged and saved the harlot in justice and mercy. (Jn.8.2-11; Is .51.7-8)

4. Let us trust in the saving grace of the Lord and follow his ways to be saved in his mercy. Amen!

SERMON NO.118/B-5

Sixteenth Sunday After Pentecost

M /EW   *Scripture Readings:*

Ps.124   Eph.6.10-18

Ex.4.10-17   Mk.9.14-29

Theme: Nothing is impossible for faith

Sermon Outline:

1   God performed wonderful deeds through Moses in Egypt and in the wilderness. (Ex.4 ff; Heb.1.23-29)

2. Disciples of Christ lacked faith to caste out the dumb spirit. (Mk.9.14-19)

3. The faithful prayers of the righteous can do wonders. (Mk.9.20-29; Jas.5.13-18)

4. With the amours of God we can overcome all evils and sorrows. (Eph.6.10-18).

Amen!

SERMON NO.119/B-53

Seventeenth Sunday After Pentecost

M/EW   *Scripture Readings:*
               Ps.126,133   1 Cor.3.1-9,18-23
               Num.11.16-17,24-29   Mk.9.30-41

Theme: Lesson of the Cross for daily life

Sermon Outline:
  1. Moses had to bear the cross of his people. (Num.11)
  2. Bearing the Cross is a humble duty. (Mk.9.33-37)
  3. A servant of the Lord must be free from jealousy. (Mk.9.38-41)
  4. Servants of God are His fellow –workers, who must serve in humility, fellowship and unity.
      Amen!

SERMON NO.120/B-54

Eighteenth Sunday After Pentecost

M /EW   *Scripture Readings:*
               Ps.127.   1 Cor.13
               Mal.2.13-15   Mk.10.2-12

Theme: The family: husband and wife

Sermon Outline:

1. God is the maker of a good family. (Mk.10.2-12; Ps.127)

2. A good family is built up in true love. (1 Cor.13)

3. God looks for godly family with godly offspring. (Mal.2.13-16)

4. Let us fear God and trust in Him to help us to build up godly families in his steadfast love and blessings. Amen!

SERMON NO.121/B-55

Nineteenth Sunday After Pentecost

M /EW   *Scripture Readings:*
                 Ps.128   Eph.6.1-4
                 Prov.4.1-9   Mk.10.13-16
                                           or
                                           Mt.18.1-14

Theme: The family: Children

Sermon Outline:

1. Children are a gift of God. (Ps.128)

2. Jesus taught that children are great in the kingdom of heaven. (Mk.10.13-16 Mt.18.1-14)

3. Children should be brought up in love and discipline. (Eph.6.1-4; Prov.4.1-9)

4. Let us pray to God to help us build up our family, and to bless our children. Amen!

SERMON NO.122/B-56

Twentieth Sunday After Pentecost

M /EW   *Scripture Readings:*
                 Ps.49   Rev.3.4-22
                 Deut.8.6-18   Mk.10.17-22

Theme: The spiritual danger of trusting in wealth

Sermon Outline:

1. God is provider of food, wealth and prosperity. (Deut.8.6-18)

2. Love of wealth and love of the world are spiritual dangers which hinder to follow and please God. (Mk.10.17-22; Rev.3.16-22; 1 Jn.2.15-17)

3. Those who love God and overcome the traits of the world shall inherit the kingdom of heaven. (Rev.3.19-22)

4. Let us pray to the Lord to help us over-come such spiritual dangers. Amen!

SERMON NO.123/B-57

Twenty –first Sunday After Pentecost

M/EW   *Scripture Readings:*
                 Ps.66   Acts.16.25-34
                 Is.35.3-10   Mk.10.46-52

Theme: Faith is the beginning of a pilgrimage

Sermon Outline:

1. The Almighty God is faithful to take care of His people. (Is.35;Ps.66)

2. Jesus gave sight to Bartimaeus seeing his faith, who followed him in gratitude and joy. (Mk.10.46-52)

3. The jailor believed in Christ, and his whole family was baptized and were saved. (Acts.16.25-34)

4. Let us continue to keep faith in the Lord until the end and be saved by his grace. (Rev.2.10c; Eph.2.8-9). Amen!

SERMON NO.124/B-58

Twenty- second Sunday After Pentecost

M /EW   *Scripture Readings:*
                 Ps.84   Eph.2.13-22
                 Jer.7.1-14   Mk.11.15-18

Theme: ***The true temple of God***

Sermon Outline:

1. The temple of God should be a house of holiness and righteousness. (Jer.7.1-14)

2. The temple of God should be a house of praise, prayer and peace. (Ps.84)

3. The temple of God should not be a house of trades and business. (Mk.11.15-18)

4. The Church of Christ is built upon the foundation of Christ, with people purified by his blood and reconciled to God and to one another. (Eph.2.13-22) Amen!

SERMON NO.125/B-59

Twenty – third Sunday After Pentecost

M /EW   *Scripture Readings:*
                 Ps.10   Rev.19.1-8
                 Jer.22.1-9   Mk.12.13-17

Theme: ***Ultimate loyalty that we owe to God***

Sermon Outline:

1. Disloyalty to God and righteous deeds bring sorrow and curse. (Jer.22.1-9)

2. Jesus taught due loyalty to God and to the national rulers. (Mk.12.13-17)

3. Our loyalty to God and righteousness shall be the fine linen garments of the Bride of the coming King, the Lamb of God. (Rev.19.1-8)

4. Let us be loyal to God and practice justice and righteousness to be blessed by the Lord now and forever. Amen!

SERMON NO.126/B-60

Twenty –fourth Sunday After Pentecost

M/EW   *Scripture Readings:*
Ps.11.161-176   1 Jn.4.13-21
or 24.1-6
Mic.6.2-8   Mk:12.28-34

Theme: The Great Commandment

Sermon Outline:

1. The Great commandment is to love God and to love one another. (Mk.12.28-34)

2. The Word of God teaches us to practice love and righteousness. (Ps.119.161-176)

3. Our love of God must be demonstrated in our love for one another. (1 Jn.4.13-21)

4. Let us be determined to love God and to love one another at all costs in following the Lord Jesus Christ. Amen!

SERMON NO.127/B-61

Twenty-sixth Sunday After Pentecost

M /EW   *Scripture Readings:*
               Ps.50.1-15   2 Cor.8.1-9
               Ex.35.20-29   Mk.12.38-44

Theme: A generous spirit

Sermon Outline:
1. God expected freewill offering from His people. (Ex.35.20-29)
2. Jesus appreciated the little offering of the poor widow. (Mk.12.38-44)
3. St.Paul encouraged churches to contribute to the relief fund liberally.
4. Let us give our offering sacrificially and avail his redeeming grace. (Ps.50.14-15) Amen!

SERMON NO.128/B-62

Twenty- eighth Sunday After Pentecost

M/EW   *Scripture Readings:*
               Ps .144   Rom.16.1-16
               Prov.31.10-31   Mk.14.3-9

Theme: The partnership in Christ of women and men

Sermon Outline:
1. Mutual support and cooperation between men and women is essential to build up a healthy family and human society. (Prov.31)
2. Jesus appreciated the costly anointing of the woman at Bethany. (Mk.14.3-9)

3. St. Paul's list of supporting the faithful early church leaders includes many couples and women. (Rom.16.1-16)

4. The church should encourage women's leadership and blessed family lives. Amen!

SERMON NO. 129/B-63

Twenty –ninth Sunday After Pentecost

M/EW   *Scripture Readings:*
          Ps.72.1-14   Rev.5.1-10
          Isa.42.1-7   Jn.18.33-37

*Theme: **The good confession made by Jesus Christ***

Sermon Outline:

1. Jesus was the promised Messiah. (Is.42)

2. Jesus confessed that he is the eternal Kings. (Jn.18.36; Lk.1.68-75; Is.9.6-7)

3. Jesus was worthy to open the seal of salvation. (Rev.5.1-10)

4. Let us praise God for His Divine plan to save the world through Christ. Amen!

CHAPTER THREE

Sermon Outlines
for YEAR C (130-195)

SERMON NO.130/C-1

Fourth Sunday Before Christmas
(Advent I)

M/EW   *Scripture Readings:*

Ps.75   2 Pet.3.8-15a

Jer.23.1-6   Lk.12.32-40

Theme: Watching for Christ in patience and hope

Sermon Outline:

1. God had promised to send the Messiah in the family of David. (Jer.23.5-6)

2. The Messiah had to come as the good shepherd. (Jer.23.1-4; Ezek.34; Jn.10.7-18)

3. The Lord is coming back soon. (Lk.12.37-40; Rev .22.7,20)

4. Let us be ready to meet the Lord and be rewarded. (Lk.12.32-36; Phil.1.9-11; Am.4.12) Amen!

SERMON NO. 131/C-2

Third Sunday Before Christmas
(Advent II)

M/EW   *Scripture Readings:*

Ps.110   Acts.3.18-26

Deut. 18.9-19   Lk.24.44-48

Theme: The Old Testament is fulfilled in Christ

Sermon Outline:

1. God's promises are certain. (Ps.110.4)

2. God had promised to send a prophet and prophets like Moses and Melchizedek. (Deut.18.13-19; Ps.110; Is.9.6; 11.1-9; Heb.5.1-10)

3. The Old Testament prophecies are fulfilled in Christ. (Lk.24.44-48; Acts .3.18-26)

4. Let us praise God for his faithfulness in keeping his promises to save us through Christ. (Is.40.1-8). Amen!

SERMON NO.132/C-3

Secondary Sunday Before Christmas
(Advent III)

M/EW   Scripture Readings:

Ps. 28   Acts. 19.1-6

Is.35   Mk .1.1-8

Theme: The Message of John the Baptist

Sermon Outline:

1. God's promises of deliverance of his people. (Ps.35)

2. John the Baptist came to prepare the way of Christ. (Mk.1.1-8)

3. It was prophesied that Jesus shall give the baptism of the Holy Spirit and fire. (Mk.1.7-8; Mt.3.11)

4. The apostles gave baptism of the Holy Spirit in the name of Christ. (Acts. 19.1-6)

5. Let us pray fervently in the name of Christ to receive the Holy Spirit, and receive power to be his witnesses. (Acts.) Amen!

SERMON NO.133/C-4

First Sunday Before Christmas
(Advent IV)

M/EW   *Scripture Readings:*

Ps.132   Heb.2.10-18

Is.49.1-6   L.k.1.39-49

Theme: At Christmas we welcome Jesus who is like us in every way apart from sin

Sermon Outline:

1. Jesus is the Son of God and the eternal Kings. (Ps.132; Is.9.6-7)

2. Jesus was born as a human child like us, more like a brother in flesh and blood. (Lk.1.39-49; Heb.2.10-18)

3. Jesus was born as a light to the nations and brought salvation to the world. (Is.49.6)

4. Jesus overcame temptations, and as a perfect high priest, he is able and merciful to help us overcoming sins. (Heb.2.15-18; 7.25; Jn.16.33; 2 Cor.5.21)

5. Let us welcome our perfect high priest, who is coming again for us; Maranatha. (1 Co.16.22) Amen !

SERMON NO.134/C-5

Christmas Day

M/EW   *Scripture Readings:*
                Ps.98   *Titus3.4-7*
                Mic.5.2-4   *Lk.2.1-16*

Theme: The birth of the saviour, who is the Word made flesh

Sermon Outline:

1. The saviour Lord Jesus was born in the blessed city of Bethlehem Ephrathah according to the promise of the father. (Mic.5.2-4; Lk.2.1-16)

2. Jesus is the Word made flesh – the Creator born as the Son of man and Son of God. (Jn.1.1-3,14)

3. Jesus, the saviour Lord is full of grace, hope and truth, who brings justification and eternal life. (Jn.1.14-18; Titus 3.4-7)

4. Let us rejoice and sing new songs in praising the Almighty God of Love who opened up the way of peace and redemption in Christ Jesus. (Ps.98) Amen!

SERMON NO.135/ C-6

First Sunday After Christmas

M/EW   Scripture Readings:
               Ps.128   Col.3.12-21
               Zech. 8.3-6   Lk.2.41-52

Theme: Family Life

Sermon Outline:

1. Jesus and his parents visited Jerusalem to worship God and to celebrate the Passover festival. (Lk.41-52; 1 Sam.1)

2. The family who faithfully worships the Lord and fears him are blessed by Him in all respects. (Ps.128; Zech.8.3-6)

3. A blessed family is full of love, peace and joy of the Lord. (Cl.8.12-12; Phil.4.4-7)

4   Let us fear the Lord, trust and worship him faithfully, and enjoy God's manifold blessings in Christ. Amen!

SERMON NO.136/C-7

New Years Day

Naming of Jesus and Renewal of the Covenant

M /EW   *Scripture Readings:*
Ps .20   Rev.10.5-13
Joel 2.28-32   Lk.2.15-21

Theme: The name of Jesus

Sermon Outline:

1. The name of Jesus was announced by the angel of God from Heaven . (Mt.1.21)

2. The name of Jesus was given in the temple of Jerusalem according to Jewish customs. (Lk.2.15-21)

3. With the coming of Jesus God's covenant was renewed. (Jer.31.31-34; Joel 2.31)

4. Those who call upon the name of Lord Jesus shall be saved. (Rom.10.13, Joel 2.31)

5. As the Day of the Lord is at hand, let us call upon the name Jesus continually and be saved. (1 Thess.5.16-18; Joel 2.32).

Amen!

SERMON NO.137/C-8

Second Sunday After Christmas The Epiphany of our Lord

M/EW   *Scripture Readings:*

Ps.47 *or* 92   Eph.3.1-12

Is.60.1-5   Mt.2.1-12

or 45.22-25

Theme: *The coming of the wise men from the east is a sign that Christ is for the whole human race*

Sermon Outline:

1. Jesus has come as the light of the world. (Is.60.1; Jn.1.4-5;8.12)

2. Seeing the star of Jesus, the light and saviour of the world, the wise men came from the east to worship him. (Mt.2.1-12; Jn.3.16; Acts 9.3-6; Eph.5-8)

3. Let us praise God and proclaim the name of Jesus, so that the world may be saved.   Amen!

SERMON NO.138/C-9

Third Sunday After Christmas
Baptism of Jesus

M /EW   *Scripture Readings:*

Ps.2   Acts 8.26-40

Is.42.1-7   Mt.3.15-22

Theme: *At His baptism Jesus was revealed as the Son of God*

Sermon Outline:

1. Jesus has come as the promised Messiah, the son of man and the Son of God. (Ps.2; Is.42)

2. At his humble baptism Jesus was declared from heaven

as the beloved Son of God. (Mt.3.15-22)

3. As the promised Messiahship was fulfilled in the life and work of Jesus, many Jews and Gentiles believed and were baptized in his name, including the Ethiopian Finance Minister. (Acts 8.26-40; 53.7-8. etc.)

4. Let us believe in the saviour Lord Jesus strongly, and prayerfully resolve to be His witnesses boldly. (Mt.28.18-20; Acts 4.2-31) Amen !

SERMON NO.139/C-10

Fourth Sunday After Christmas

M/EW   *Scripture Readings:*
                 Ps. 145   Gal.3.23-29
                 Is.25.6-9   Jn.2.1-11

Theme: ***Jesus brings joy through the fulfillment of God's gracious purpose***

Sermon Outline:

1. Jesus brought joy in the wedding feast at Cana miraculously. (Jn. 2.1-11)

2. God's wonder working grace and power are demonstrated through Christ Jesus. (Ps.145; Jn.5.19-23)

3   Christians, in following Christ, should put on Christ, and practice love, joy and peace. (Gal.3.23-29)

4   Let us trust in the Lord Jesus and follow him. Amen!

SERMON NO.140/C-11

Republic Day

M /EW   *Scripture Readings:*
                 Ps. 85   1 Pet. 2.11-16
                 Neh.5.14-19   Mt.22.14-21

Theme: Patriotism

Sermon Outline:

1. Nehemiah was a faithful statesman. (Neh.5.14-19)

2. Christians should be good citizens-submissive and faithful to the rulers and to the law of the land. (Mt.22.15-21; 1 Pet.2.11-16)

3. We must pray and be involved in bringing peace and prosperity in our country and in the whole world. (Ps.85; 2 Chr.7.14)   Amen !

SERMON NO.141/C-12

Fifth Sunday After Christmas

M /EW   *Scripture Readings:*
                  Ps .123   Acts.5.12-16
                  2 Kings.5.1-14   Mk. 1. 40-45

Theme: God suffers with all those who suffer in this world

Sermon Outline:

1. God healed Naaman, the leper miraculously. (2 Kings.5.1-14)

2. Jesus was kind enough to heal the lepers. (Mk.1.40-45)

3. The apostles healed many sick people in the name of Christ. (Acts.5.12-16)

4. Let us pray for the sick to be healed in the name of Christ, so that his name may be glorified.   Amen!

SERMON NO. 142/C-13

Sixth Sunday After Christmas

M/EW   *Scripture Readings:*
                  Ps.122   1 Cor.3.10-17
                  Hag.2.1-9   Jn.2.13-22

Theme: The true temple of God is the Church, the Body of Christ

Sermon Outline:

1. God had promised that the later temple shall have greater splendour and prosperity. (Hag.2.1-9)

2. Jesus attempted to cleanse the temple of Jerusalem. (Jn.2.13-22)

3. St. Paul taught that the church is the body of Christ and the holy temple of God. (1 Cor.3.10-17; 12.2-13)

4. As a true temple of God, let us continue to worship him in truth and in spirit. Amen !

SERMON NO.143/C-14

Seventh Sunday After Christmas

M/EW   *Scripture Readings:*

Ps.113   Jas.2.1-9

Am.9. 5-10   Lk.4.16-30

Theme: God has no favorites. His love is for all

Sermon Outline:

1. God is an impartial judge and King. (Am.9.5-10; 1 Cor.14.33; Jas. 2.1-9)

2. God is concerned for the poor and the righteous for his glory. (Lk.4. 16-30)

3. Let us praise God for his steadfast and impartial love and concern for us, and make efforts to be worthy of him Amen!

SERMON NO.144/C-15

Eighth Sunday After Christmas
(Same as the twenty–fifth Sunday After Pentecost)

SERMON NO.145/C-16

Ninth Sunday Before Easter

M /EW   *Scripture Readings:*
                 Ps.8   1 Pet.3.1-7
                 Gen.2.4b-8, 18-25   Gal.3.23-29
                                         Mk.10.2-9

Theme: ***God creates men and women to be joint heirs of his Kingdom***

Sermon Outline:

1. God has kept all things under the rule of Christ. (Ps.8; Gen 1 &2 ; Heb.2; Mt.28.18)

2. God has made men and women to be his stewards, and to inherit His Kingdom. (Mk.10.2-9; Gal 3.23-29)

3. Men and women should put on Christ, be submissive to one another, and give glory to God. (1 Pet.3.1-7; 1 Cor.11.2-16)

4. Let us praise God for all His gracious plans and purposes, and participate in His task faithfully to inherit His Kingdom. Amen !

SERMON NO.146/C-17

Eighth Sunday Before Easter

M/EW   *Scripture Readings:*
                Ps. 51.1-17   Rom.7.15-8.2.
                Jer.17.5-10   Mk.7.14-23

Theme: ***Only by the grace of God can our hearts be made pure***

Sermon Outline:

1. Man is born in sin. So he fails to do good.(Ps.51.1-5; Jer 17.5-10; Rom.7)

2. Man's sinful nature is revealed by his evil thoughts, words and works. (Mk.7.14-23; Jas.1.14-15; Num.32.23)

3. Christ alone has overcome sins, and can give us victory and freedom from sins and make our heart pure. (2 Cor.5.21; Heb 2.17-18; Rom.8.2)

4. Let us praise God, for there is no condemnation for those who are in Christ Jesus. (Rom.8.1; 6.23)   Amen!

SERMON NO.147/C-18

Seventh Sunday Before Easter

M/EW   *Scripture Readings:*
              Ps.6   Acts.26.12-20
              Ezek.18.25-32   Lk.15.1-2,11-32

Theme: God has promised forgiveness to the penitent

Sermon Outline:

1. God has promised to give new heart and new spirit to the penitent. (Ezek.18.25-32)

2. The father forgave his prodigal son. (Lk. 15)

3. St. Paul's personal testimony of God's forgiveness and renewal in Christ Jesus. (Acts.26.12-20)

4. Let us come to the Lord in penitence and trust to be forgiven and have victory over sins and sorrows. Amen!

SERMON NO.148/C-19

Ash Wednesday

M/EW   *Scripture Readings:*
              Ps.32   1 Cor.9.24-27
              Is.58.1-9a   Mt.6.1-6, 16-18

Theme: The spirit of Christian discipline

Sermon Outline:

1. Sin brings pain in the body and mind of a sinner. (Ps.32.3-4)

2. Repentance and confession of sins brings forgiveness, peace, and blessings. (Ps.1-2,5-11)

3. St. Paul has advised to practice self- discipline for overcoming Christian life. (1 Cor.9.24-27)

4. Let us pray and fast humbly and repentantly, so that we may be forgiven and grow in Christ. (Mt.6, 1 Pet .2.1-12) Amen!

SERMON NO.149/C-20

Sixth Sunday before Easter

M/EW   *Scripture Readings:*
              Ps.160.1-23   Heb.4.4-16
              Deut.6.10-18   Lk.4.1-13

Theme: The victory of Jesus helps us when we are tempted

Sermon Outline:

1. The Israelites failed to trust in God and were destroyed in the wilderness. (Heb.4.4-6)

2. God looks for man's honour, full surrender and total obedience to bless him graciously and miraculously. (Deut.6.10-18)

3. Jesus had victory over Satan due to his full surrender to the Father. (Lk.4.1-13)

4. Jesus can give victory over sin and temptations to those who draw near to him in faith and penitence. (Heb.2.17-18; 4.7-16)

5. Let us come to the Lord in faith and penitence and enjoy his grace and mercy. Amen!

SERMON NO.150/C-21

Fifth Sunday Before Easter

M/EW   *Scripture Readings:*

Ps .57   Rom.8.31-39

Hos.14.1-8   Lk.36-50

Theme: *The compassionate love of God gives confidence to his children*

Sermon Outline:

1. God has promised long before to forgive and save his people. (Hos.14.1-8; Ps. 57.70)

2. Jesus forgives the sins of those who repent. (Lk.7.36-50)

3. Let us believe and trust that nothing can separate us from the love of God through Christ Jesus. (Rom.8.31-39) Amen!

SERMON NO.151/C-22

Fourth Sunday Before Easter

M/EW   *Scripture Readings:*

Ps.99   2 Cor.4.1-5

Ex.22.12-23   Lk.9.28-36

Theme: *True glory of God is manifested in the humanity of Jesus*

Sermon Outline:

1. God's glory was present with Moses on Mt. Sinai. (Ex.33.12-23; Ps .99.5-7)

2. Jesus was full of the glory of God during his transfiguration. (Lk.9.28-36)

3. Jesus was full of the glory of God. (2 Cor. 4.1-6; Jn.14-18)

4. Let us praise God for his assurance to give us his glory through Christ now, and forever, in heaven. (Col.3.4) Amen!

SERMON NO.152/C-23

Third Sunday Before Easter

M/EW   *Scripture Readings:*

Ps. 76   Acts. 19.11-20

Is. 49.22-26   Lk.11.14-26

Theme: The power of God is manifested in the works of Jesus

Sermon Outline:

1. God is Almighty, majestic and terrible. (Ps.76)

2. God has revealed that the powerful kings and rich shall honour and serve his people. (Is.22-26)

3. Jesus' earthly ministry was full of God's power and authority. (Lk.11.14-26; Mk.2.12; Jn.2.11; Is.49.1-4)

4. Let us praise God for his wonderful works through Jesus, our Lord and saviour. Amen!

SERMON NO.153/C-24

Second Sunday Before Easter

M/EW   *Scripture Readings:*

Ps.66   Heb.5.1-10

Is.53.1-12   Jn.12.20-36a

Theme: The magnetism of the Cross

Sermon Outline:

1. Christ was the promised Messiah and the suffering servant of God Jehovah. (Is .53.1-12)

2. Christ is the eternal high priest in the order of Melchizedeck. (Heb.5.1-10)

3. Christ Jesus suffered and died on the cross for the world in obedience to the Father. (Is.53.1-12; Jn.12.20-36a)

4. Let us follow the Lord Jesus in total obedience to him , who is the saviour as well as the light of the world, so

that we may be saved and be rewarded by the Father. (Jn.12.35-36; 2 Tim.2.10-13; Col.31-40) Amen!

SERMON NO.154/C-25

First Sunday Before Easter Palm Sunday

M/EW   *Scripture Readings:*

Ps 69.1-21   1 Cor.1.18-25

Is.50.4-10   Lk.22.1-23.56

or 23.1-49

(Procession: Lk.19.9-40)

Theme: Christ enters Jerusalem to offer his life for salvation of the world

Sermon Outline:

1. The eternal King's humble procession for enthronement in fulfillment of the scriptures. (Lk.19.29-40; Ps.118.26; Is. 62.11; Zech.9.9)

2. Christ Jesus, the eternal King, offers himself to save the world in humble obedience to the Father. (Lk.19-23; Is.50.4-10)

3. The Word of the Cross is the power of God for our salvation. (1Cor.1.18; Rom.1.16-17)

4. Let us humbly believe and boldly proclaim the Christ crucified, who alone is the saviour and the pride of the world. (1 Cor.1.18-25,30-31) Amen!

SERMON NO.155/C-26

Monday Before Easter
Passion (Holy) Week

M/EW   *Scripture Readings:*

Ps.27.2-5, 13-14   Lk. 19.41-48

Is.42.1-7

Theme: Cleansing of the temple of Jerusalem

Sermon Outline:

1. God sent Jesus His Son into the world as a covenant to his people and the light to the nations. (Is.5.1-7; 42.6; Lk.20.9-19; Jn.6.32-40; 8.12; 10.10-11)

2. Jesus taught in the temple and drove out the traders, as it was a house of prayer. (Lk. 19.45-47; Is.56.7; Jer .7.11)

3   The selfish and wicked Jewish leaders sought to kill Jesus. (Lk.19.47-48)

4. Let us sincerely pray to the Lord to cleanse our hearts and our church, and to make us the true temple of God, the house of prayer. (1 Cor.3.16) Amen!

SERMON NO.156/C-27

Tuesday Before Easter
Passion (Holy) Week

M/EW   *Scripture Readings:*
Ps. 71.1-2,9-12   Mk.14.1-9
Is.49.1-7

Theme: The Anointing of Jesus

Sermon Outline:

1. Jesus' anointing by a woman with costly oil and penitent tears. (Mk.14.1-9)

2. People's indignance and criticism. (Mk.14-7; Lk.7.36-50)

3. Jesus' joy of His anointing before death. (Mk.14.6-9)

4. Jesus blessed the woman, forgave her and announced his death. (Mk.14.Lk.7)

5. Let us worship the Lord with repentance and gratitude, and pay homage to him thankfully. Amen!

SERMON NO.157/C-28

Wednesday Before Easter
Passion (Holy) Week

M/EW   *Scripture Readings:*
              Ps.55.12-13,20-22   Is.50.4-10
              Mt.26.1-5,14-16

Theme: Judas Iscariot betrays Jesus

Sermon Outline:

1.   The Jewish leaders planned to kill Jesus. (Mk.26.1-5)

2.   Judas received money to betray Jesus. (Mt.26.14-15)

3.   It is usual for the servants of God to suffer for the sake of His kingdom. (Ps.55.Is.50.4-10; Phil.1.29-30)

4.   Those who betray and persecute the servants of God are bound to be cursed and to suffer. (Mt.26.24,74; Ps,16-21; Acts.1.17-20)

5.   Let us resolve to follow Jesus and be blessed, rather than following Judas and be cursed. Amen!

SERMON NO.158/C-29

Thursday Before Easter
Passion (Holy) Week
Maunday Thursday (LS)

M /EW   *Scripture Readings:*
               Ps.116   1 Cor.11.23-29
               Ex.12.1-8,11-14   Jn.13.1-17, 34-38
               or Jer.31.31-34

*Theme: **Jesus gives his disciples a new commandment and institutes the Lord's Supper***

Sermon Outline:

1. Jesus replaced the Passover feast with the Lord's Supper and gave the new covenant. (Ex.12.1-14; Jer.31.31-34; Jn.13.1-17)

2. Jesus is the Bread of life from heaven. (Jn.6.31-34)

3. Let us observe the Lord's Supper with repentance and confidence to receive eternal life through Christ. (1 Cor.11.23-30; Jn.6.35-40)   Amen!

SERMON NO.159/C-30

Good Friday

M/EW   *Scripture Readings:*
                     Ps. 88   Heb. 10.4-21
                     Ex. 12.21-33, 40-42   Jn. 18.1-19.43
                                               or 19.1-37

Theme: The Victory of the Cross

Sermon Outline:

1. The Passover Lamb is replaced by Jesus the Lamb of God for the redemption of the world. (Ex..12;21-33; Jn.1.29)

2. Jesus' offering on the Cross was the sacrifice once and for all

    (Jn.19; Heb.10.)

3. Let us trust in the Lord Jesus, who offered his life for us, and surrender at his feet until the end to receive eternal life and boundless peace in Heaven. Amen!

SERMON NO.160/C-31

Easter Sunday

M/EW   *Scripture Readings:*
                     Ps .118   Col.3.1-4
                     Ex.15.1-2, 19-21   Jn.20.1-18
                                               or Lk.24.13-35

Theme: The Lord is risen, he is risen indeed, Alleluyah!

Sermon Outline:

1. God redeemed his people from the Egyptian bondage graciously and miraculously. (Ex.15)

2   God raised Jesus His Son from the dead wonderfully, and opened up the way for his faithful to overcome death in Christ according to His promises. (Jn.20;Lk.24: Ps.16.10; 23.6; 118.17; Isa.25.8; 1Cor.15.)

3. Jesus' triumphant resurrection as the first fruit among the dead assures our resurrection. (1 Cor.15.20-58).

4. The faithful believers and followers of Christ Jesus are already lifted up into the heaven in him spiritually, hence they must have heavenly life and action while on earth, as risen people. (Col.3.1-4; Phil.2.20; 2 Cor.5.17; Rom.6.1-11)

5. Let us trust and follow that risen Lord, who has risen indeed, so that we might arise now spiritually and at the end physically by his grace and mercy. Amen!

SERMON NO.161/C-32

First Sunday After Pentecost

M /EW   *Scripture Readings:*
               Ps.114   Rev.1.9-20
               Acts.5.12-16   Jn.20.19-31

Theme: Joy and peace, power and new life are given through the resurrection of Christ

Sermon Outline:

1. Our God is a wonder working God. (Ps.114)

2. The resurrection of Christ has wonderfully brought joy and peace, power and new life for his believers and followers. (Jn.20.19-31)

3. The apostles healed and gave new life to many in the name of the risen Lord, who is seated at the right hand of the father in Heavenly power and glory. (Acts. ; Rev.1.9-20)

4. Let us praise God for our risen Lord and saviour Jesus Christ, surrender our lives before him, and avail all the blessings through him.(Mt.11.28-30) Amen!

SERMON NO.162/C-33

Second Sunday After Easter

M /EW   *Scripture Readings:*
                 Ps.126   1 Cor.15.1-11
                 Acts.3.11-18   Jn.21.1-14

Theme: Witness to Christ's resurrection

Sermon Outline:

1. The wonder working God always gives gracious rewards beyond imagination. (Ps.126)

2. The risen Lord's gracious visions to his disciples. (Jn.20-21)

3. The disciple's making the lame man walk in the name of Christ was a witness to his resurrection. (Acts.3.11-18)

4. Let us believe in the risen Lord and be his witnesses. Amen!

SERMON NO.163/C-34

Third Sunday After Easter

M /EW   *Scripture Readings:*
                 Ps. 23   Rev.7.9-17
                 Acts.9.32-43   Jn.10.22-30

Theme: The Good Shepherd

Sermon Outline:

1   King David proclaimed that the Lord is our shepherd. (Ps.23)

2.   Jesus is the good shepherd coming down from Heaven in fulfillment of the Lord's promises. (Jn.10; Rev.7.9-17; Ezk 34.16)

3.   Jesus as the good shepherd gives his life for his sheep, washes them with his blood, gives them eternal life, and becomes their shepherd for ever. (Rev.7.9-17)

4.   Tabitha received back her life in the name of Christ, the good shepherd. (Acts .9.32-43)

5.   Let us follow our good shepherd the Lord Jesus, and rejoice in Him. Amen!

SERMON NO.164/C-35

Fourth Sunday After Easter

M/EW   *Scripture Readings:*

Ps. 96   Rev.21.22.27

Acts .14.21-27   Jn.151-11

Theme: Our redemption is completed through life in union with Christ

Sermon Outline:

1.   Jesus' parable of the true vine clearly explains the fruitfulness of intimate relationship with Christ. (Jn. 15.1-11)

2.   Intimate relationship and spiritual union with Christ may also involve tribulations and sufferings for his kingdom. (Acts.14.21-27;2 Tim.11-13; Phil.1.-29-30)

3.   Let us live in intimate relationship with Christ and serve him at all costs, and prepare for our eternal life and heavenly blessings. (Rom.6.23; Phil.2.12-13) Amen!

SERMON NO.165/C-36

Fifth Sunday After Easter

M /EW   *Scripture Readings:*
                   Ps. 67   Rev.22.1-5
                   Acts.15.22-31   Jn.15.26-16.7

Theme: The Spirit of truth and love is promised to the Church

Sermon Outline:

1. Jesus promised to give the spirit of truth and love to his people to guide and comfort them. (Jn.15.26-16.7)

2. The Holy Spirit guided and supported the Church dynamically. (Acts.15.22.-31)

3. The faithful followers of the Lord Jesus have been promised with eternal and glorious life in heaven. (Rev.22.1-5; Col.3.1-5)

4. Let us continue to pray and follow Christ, so that he might guide and support us in our daily lives and actions until we are lifted up to the heavenly glory. Amen!

SERMON NO.166/C-37

Ascension Day

M/EW   *Scripture Readings:*
                   Ps.21.1-6,13   Acts.1.1-11
                   Dan.7.9-10,13-14   Mt.28.16-20
                                             or Lk.24.44-53

Theme: The Son of man is exalted to the right hand of God

Sermon Outline:

1. The exaltation of the Son of man to the right hand of God in Heaven is a fulfillment of His Promises. (Dan.7.9-14; Ps.21; Heb.1.1-4)

2. Jesus as the Son of Man and Son of God was lifted up to the right hand of the Father in Heaven. (Acts.1.11; Acts 2.33 Mt 3.17; 17.9, 22-23)

3. Let us praise God for His gracious Divine plan to lift us up to the high and the holy heavens with Christ in his second coming. (Jn.14.1-6; 2 Tim.2.11-13). Amen !

SERMON NO. 167/C-38

Sixth Sunday After Easter

M/EW   *Scripture Readings:*
            Ps.84   Rev.21.1-7
            Acts.18.1-11   Jn.17.20-26

Theme: We are created to know God and to abide in him

Sermon Outline:

1. Jesus prayed to the Father for his disciples to be with him in the glorious heaven eternally. (Jn.17.20-26)

2. The people of God should worship him faithfully in joy and sorrows, abide in Him and grow from strength to strength heaven ward. (Ps.84; Jn.15)

3. Let us realize the love and grace of God and abide in him and share his eternal heavenly glory. Amen !

SERMON NO.168/C-39

Seventh Sunday After Easter

The Pentecost

M/EW   *Scripture Readings:*
            Ps.139   Acts.2.1-11
            Is.44.1-5   Jn. 20.19-33

Theme: The gift of the Holy Spirit

Sermon Outline:

1. God fulfilled his promises to send the Holy Sprit and to spread his kingdom through his work. (Is. 44.1-5; Acts.2.1-11; Joel.2.28-29)

2. The Holy Spirit searches all things, and guides, supports and comforts his people wonderfully. (Ps.139; Acts)

3. The Lord Jesus gave the Holy Spirit and peace to his disciples to believe and follow him faithfully and boldly, and to be his witnesses. (Jn.20.19-33; Acts.)

4. Let us pray to the Lord for the gifts, fruits, power and comforts of the Holy Spirit, and do his will and be witnesses. (1 Cor.12-14; Gal.2.22-23; Eph.4; Acts) Amen!

Sermon No. 169/C-40

First Sunday After Pentecost

Trinity Sunday

M/EW   *Scripture Readings:*
                  Ps . 93   Rom.8.1-11
                  1 Kings 8.22-29   Jn.14.8-11

Theme: God the Holy Trinity

Sermon Outline:

1. The Lord Jehovah is the Almighty God Israel and the only True God of all. (1 Kings 8.22-29; 1 Cor.8.4-6)

2. Jesus promised to pray to the Father to send the Counsellor, who is the Spirit of truth. (Jn.148-17; 16.26-27)

3. God- the Father, Jesus- the Son, and Holy Spirit the Counsellor work together. (Rom.8.1-11; Gen.1.1-3, 26; Mt.1-4; Lk.1-4; etc)

4. Let us humbly believe in the Holy Trinity as revealed in the Holy Bible, and proclaim it. Amen!

SERMON NO.170/C-41

Second Sunday After Pentecost

M/EW   *Scripture Readings:*

Ps.94.1-15   Rom.11.33-12.2

Am.6.1-8   Lk.6.17-26

Theme: The difference between the world values and what God values

Sermon Outlines:

1. God is always the Rock of refuge for the righteous and the poor. (Is.94)

2. Jesus proclaimed the good days for the people under poverty and exploitation. (Lk.6.17-26; 4.18-19)

3. God's wisdom, ways and judgments are different from the world's. (Rom.11.33-12.2; Is .55.8-9; 1 Jn. 2.15-17)

4. Let us resolve to walk in the ways of the Lord and ask his blessings. (Gen.17.1-2; Rom.12.1-2; Eph.5.15-20). Amen!

SERMON NO.171/C-42

Third Sunday After Pentecost

M /EW   *Scripture Readings:*

Ps. 13   Rom.12.9-21

1 Sam.24.8-22   Lk.6.27-36

Theme: Evil can only be overcome with good

Sermon Outline:

1. Evil power threatens to weaken the faith of the righteous. (Ps.13)

2. King Saul sought to kill David, but David honoured him as God's anointed king, and spared his life. (1 Sam.24.8-22)

3. Those who love their enemies and help the needy shall be rewarded by God abundantly. (Lk.6.27-36; Rom.12.9-21; Mt.5.20; Jas.1.26-27)

4. Let us follow the Lord and overcome the evil with good. (Rom.12.21) Amen!

SERMON NO. 172/C-43

Fourth Sunday After Pentecost

M/EW   *Scripture Readings:*
                  Ps.41   Rom.14.1-13
                  Job.19.1-6.21-29   Lk.6.37-42

Theme: Judge not, and you will not be judged

Sermon Outline:

1. God is the righteous and impartial judge of all. (Job.19)

2. The Lord Jesus taught not to judge one another. (Lk.6.37-42; Mt.7.1-5; Rom.12.14.10-12)

3. Let us strive to be exemplary and caring than becoming a stumbling block before the weak.   Amen!

SERMON NO. 173/C-44

Fifth Sunday After Pentecost

M/EW   *Scripture Readings:*
                  Ps.111   Acts.10.30-43
                  Is.52.7-10   Lk.11-23

Theme: The works of Jesus are signs of his being Christ

Sermon Outline:

1. The Lord God is always majestic, righteous and gracious. (Ps.111)

2. The coming Messiah was promised by God to save his people miraculously, to startle the nations, and to be exalted. (Is.52.7-10)

3. Jesus proved his divine messiahship, even by giving life to the dead, as was at Nain and Bethany. (Lk.7.11-23; Jn.11)

4. Jesus graciously saved the Gentiles and the untouchables even through his disciples and apostles. (Acts.10; 20)

5. Jesus' divine activities were the signs of Christ, the anointed Messiah and saviour of the world. Praise God and trust in him. Amen!

SERMON NO.174/C-45

Sixth Sunday After Pentecost

M/EW   *Scripture Readings:*
                  Ps.129   Col.1.24-29
                  Dan.3.13-28   Lk.9.18-27

Theme: Those who confess that Jesus is the Christ must be ready to suffer

Sermon Outline:

1. The golden image and trials of faith in Babylon. (Dan.3)

2. Christ suffered to save the world. (Lk.9.27-29)

3. Our faith must be genuine and strong. (Lk.9.18-27; Col.1.24-29)

4. St. Paul confessed and proclaimed the gospel of Christ, suffered for his sake, and has set an example before us. (Col.1.18-26)

5. We must boldly confess that Jesus is Christ and be prepared to suffer for him. (Lk.9.23-27; Phil.1.29-30) Amen!

SERMON NO.175/C-46

Seventh Sunday After Pentecost

M/EW   *Scripture Readings:*
                Ps.48   Phil.1.3-18
                Is.12   Lk.10.1-12,17-20

Theme: The joy of the Lord's messengers

Sermon Outline:

1. Jesus' disciples returned after their successful gospel campaign. (Lk.10)

2. St Paul appreciates the Gospel works of the Philippian Church. (Phil.1.3-18)

3. It is a great joy to be a messenger of the gospel of peace and salvation through the Lord Jesus Christ. (Is.12; Lk.10; 1 Cor.9.16)

4. Let us resolve to be the messengers of our Lord and his gospel at all costs. (Mt.5.1-16; Lk.4.43; 1 Cor.9.16-27; 2 Tim.4.1-6)   Amen!

SERMON NO. 176/C-47

Eight Sunday After Pentecost

M/EW   *Scripture Readings:*
                Ps.112   Jas.2.14-26
                Job.29.1,7-16   Lk.10.25-37

Theme: Who is my neighbour ?

Sermon Outline:

1. Job was a righteous and very responsible neighbor. (Job.29)

2. Jesus taught that that the untouchable Samaritan trader was a good neighbour. (Lk.10.25-37; Mk.12.31)

3. Let us help one another sacrificially and make ourselves good neighbours. Amen!

SERMON NO.177/C-48

Ninth Sunday After Pentecost

M/EW   *Scripture Readings:*
              Ps.63.1-8   Phil.3.7-14
              Prov.3.11-20   Lk.10.38-42

*Theme: **The one thing necessary is God himself***

Sermon Outline:

1. Jesus appreciated Mary's preference to sit near him to hear his words than to assist Martha to prepare food. (Lk.10.38-42)

2. St. Paul emptied himself, and pressed on to know Christ and to share all the blessings and glorious rewards through Him. (Phil.3.7-14)

3. King David sought God, to proclaim his greatness and to live near him eternally. (Ps.63;73.28;23.6)

4. Let us make God our goal, refuge, strength and salvation now and forever. Amen!

SERMON NO.178/C-49

Tenth Sunday After Pentecost

M/EW   *Scripture Readings:*
              Ps.116   1 Jn.5.13-21
              Gen.18.20-33   L.k.11.1-13

Theme: "Lord, teach us to pray"

Sermon Outline:

1. Abraham's prayer. (Gen.18.20-33)

2. Most of the Psalms are prayers for deliverance, and thanksgiving for God's steadfast love. (Ps.116; etc.)

3. Jesus' prayerful life and work led the disciples to request him to teach them how to pray. (Lk.11.1-13; 1 Jn.5.13-21; Mt. 6; Mk.10.38)

4. Even today, we must ask Jesus to teach us how to pray. Amen!

SERMON NO.179/C-50

Eleventh Sunday After Pentecost

M/EW   *Scripture Readings:*
                Ps.78.1-17   Acts.7.30-41
                Is.28.9-16   Lk.11.7-32

Theme: ***Gods reveals his saving purpose through the signs which he sends***

Sermon Outline:

1. God revealed his saving purpose to Moses from the burning bush. (Acts.7.30-41; Ex.3.; Jer.1.11-19)

2. Jesus often referred to the sign of Jonah to reveal and prophesy his resurrection and the Day of judgment. (Lk.11.29-30)

3. God usually reveals, guides, and saves his people through signs and wonders. (Is.28.9-16; Ps.78)

4. Let us pray to the Lord for signs and wonders for the successful pilgrimage in our life of faith, witness and salvation. Amen!

SERMON NO.180/C-51

Twelfth Sunday After Pentecost

M/EW   *Scripture Readings:*
                Ps. 49   1 Cor.6.5-11
                Gen.13.2-12   Lk.12.13-21

Theme:　The right attitude to possessions

Sermon Outline:

1. Abraham followed the Lord faithfully, and God multiplied his possessions abundantly; while Abraham had no greed, but he practiced generosity. (Gen.13-14)

2. Jesus taught that seeking the kingdom of God is more precious and promising than the earthly riches, which are futile and corruptible. (Lk.12.13-21; 1 Cor.5-11)

3. The greedy, proud and self-righteous rich man was proved to have been fool, and had a pathetic end. (Lk.12.12-21; 16.19-31; Jas.5.1-6; 1 Jn.2.15-17; Rev.3.17-18)

4. Let us trust in the Lord for everything; and seek his kingdom and righteousness, so that he may fulfill his Divine purpose in our lives for his own glory. Amen !

SERMON NO.181/C-52

Thirteenth Sunday After Pentecost

M/EW　　　　*Scripture Readings:*

Ps.125　　　　　　　　Acts.20.17-38

Ezek.3.16-21　　　　　Lk.12.14-48

Theme:　The watchfulness that is required in the church's Pastors

Sermon Outline:

1. A pastor is a responsible messenger of God like Ezekiel. (Ezek.3.16-21; 1 &2 Tim.)

2. Jesus' parable of the faithful and the unfaithful stewards. (Lk.12.41-48)

3. St.Paul's instructions to the Pastors as the guardians of the people of God. (Acts.20.17-38)

4. The churches' Pastors must be watchful and faithful stewards of God. Amen!

SERMON NO.182/C-53

Fourteenth Sunday After Pentecost

M/EW   *Scripture Readings:*
              Ps.106.1-12,19-27   Gal.4.1-11
              Num.14.1-10a   Lk.13.10-17

Theme: God has called us to be free

Sermon Outline:

1. The ungrateful Israelites disbelieved and doubted the powerful hand of God in the wilderness. (Num.14.)

2. Jesus freed a woman from a spirit of infirmity even on a Sabbath. (Lk.13.10-17; Jn.5& 9)

3. God wishes to redeem his people from legalism, all evils, troubles and sorrows. (Gal.4.1-11; Ezek.34f; Jn.3, 8, 10)

4. We are called to be the children of God in Christ Jesus. (Gal.4.1-11; Jn.1.12-13)

5. Let us praise God and enjoy His Sonship and freedom in Christ. Amen!

SERMON NO.183/C-54

Fifteenth Sunday After Pentecost

M/EW   *Scripture Readings:*
              Ps.119.41-56   Acts.13.41-52
              1 Sam.15.10-23   Lk.14.15-24

Theme: Our responses to the call of God.

Sermon Outline:

1. God repented for King Saul's disobedience. (1 Sam.15,10-23)

2. When the invitees failed to attend, others were called to the banquet. (Lk.14.15-24)

3. When the chosen race, the Jews rejected the Gospel of Christ, the Gentiles were welcome, and they were blessed graciously and abundantly. (Acts.13.41-52)

4. Let us receive the Lord's invitation and his blessings whole-heartedly, and praise and worship him eternally. (Mt.11.28-30; Rev.3.19-22)   Amen!

SERMON NO.184/C-55

Sixteenth Sunday After Pentecost

M/EW   *Scripture Readings:*
              Ps.34.11-22   1 Thess.3.1-8
              Josh.24.14-25   Lk.14.25-33

Theme: The Cost of discipleship

Sermon Outline:

1. Joshua boldly declared that he and his family should worship the Lord Jehovah, and soon others followed them. (Josh.24.14-25)

2. Jesus taught that his discipleship is costly. (Lk.14.25-33)

3. St. Paul was comforted at the strong faith of the Thessalonian Church. (1 Thess.3.1-8)

4. Let us stand fast in the Lord until the end at all costs, for the rewards are greater in Heaven. (Mt.5.11-12; Phil.1.9-11)   Amen!

SERMON NO.185/C-56

Seventeenth Sunday After Pentecost

M/EW   *Scripture Readings:*
              Ps. 130   Phil.7-20
              Hos.11.1-11   Lk.15.1-10

Theme: ***God does not abandon his people when they go astray***

Sermon Outline:

1. The gracious God did not abandon the Israelites in spite of their unbelief and sins, although He kept them under heavy yokes to repent. (Hos.11.1-11)

2. Jesus taught that there is more joy in heaven when sinners repent. (Lk.15.1-7)

3. God looks for repentance and reconciliation than rejections, separation and condemnation. (Phil.7-20)

4. Let us praise God for His Steadfast love, and maintain loving and cordial relationship with God and with one another. Amen!

SERMON NO.186/C-57

Eighteenth Sunday After Pentecost

M /EW   *Scripture Readings:*
                 Ps.53   1 Tim.6.6-12,17-19
                 2 Kings.5.19b-27   Lk.16.1-13

Theme: ***Common sense as well as devotion are needed for the service of God***

Sermon Outline:

1. Gehazi lost his common sense and devotion due to his lustful greed. (2 Kings.5.19b-27; 1 Jn.2.15-17)

2. Jesus taught that the faithful and wise people shall succeed. (Lk.16.1-13)

3. St.Paul advised Timothy to fight a good fight for faith. (1 Tim.6.12)

4. Let us rejoice in the Lord for all his blessings, and serve him faithfully. (Rom.12.11; Phil.4.4-7)   Amen!

SERMON NO.187/C-58

Nineteenth Sunday After Pentecost

M/EW   *Scripture Readings:*

Ps.82   1Jn.3.11-22

Am.8.4-10   Lk.16.19-31

Theme: True compassion is based on justice

Sermon Outline:

1. God punishes the unjust and wicked people. (Am.8. 4-10)

2. The proud and unkind rich man proved himself a fool and was thrown into throw hell fire. (Lk.16.19-31)

3. St. John taught that one who hates his brother is a murderer, and cannot receive eternal life. (1 Jn. 3.11-22)

4. God is righteous, just and kind. Let us love and obey him, and enjoy his grace and mercy through Christ. Amen!

SERMON NO.188/C-59

Twentieth Sunday After Pentecost

M/EW   *Scripture Readings:*

Ps.138   Eph.5.15-20

Deut.26.1-11   Lk.17.11-19

Theme: Thankfulness for God's mercies

Sermon Outline:

1. The Israelites were taught to give thanks offering to the God of grace and mercies regularly for his good gifts. (Deut.26.1-11)

2. Jesus was pleased with the grateful Samaritan leper. (Lk.17.11-19)

3. St. Paul taught the people of God to always praise him whole- heartedly by singing psalms and spiritual hymns. (Eph.5.15-20)

4. Let us realize the mercies of God through Christ, and offer hearty thanks and thanks offering gratefully. Amen!

SERMON NO.189/C-60

Twenty–first Sunday After Pentecost

M/EW   *Scripture Readings:*
              Ps.61   Eph.6.10-20
              Ex.17.8-12   Lk.18.1-8

Theme: Perseverance in prayer

Sermon Outline:

1. God heard the prayers of Moses and gave them victory over the Amalekites. (Ex.17.8-12)

2. Jesus taught for perseverance in prayer to receive compassionate answer. (Lk.18.1-8)

3. St. Paul taught that we must put on the whole armour of God, and pray all times in the Spirit. (Eph.6.10-20)

4. God answers prayers. Let us be faithful and prayerful people of God. Amen!

SERMON NO.190/C-61

Twenty–second Sunday After Pentecost

M /EW   *Scriptures Readings:*
              Ps.34.1-10   1 Cor.12.12-27
              Gen.11.1-9   Lk.18.9-14

Theme: True humility is to know what we are in the sight of God

Sermon Outline:

1. God destroyed the works of man's pride. (Gen.11.1-9)

2. Jesus taught that the prayers of a self-righteous person is not heard by God. (Lk.18.9-14)

3. Since we were baptized into one body of Christ, we must maintain love and unity in true humility. (1 Cor.12.12-27)

4. Let us humble ourselves in the sight of God, and practice love and unity in the Church of Christ. (1 Pet.5.6-11; Eph.4.1-16) Amen!

SERMON NO.191/C-62

Twenty-third Sunday After Pentecost

M/EW   *Scripture Readings:*
                Ps.33.6-66   2 Cor. 12.1-10
                Jonah 3.10-4.11   Lk.19.1-10

Theme: ***God works in unexpected ways to fulfill his purpose***

Sermon Outline:

1. God saved Nineveh on their repentance beyond the expectation of Jonah. (Jonah 3-4)

2. Jesus brought salvation to the house of repentant Zechaeus. (Lk.19.1-10)

3. St.Paul saw that when we are humble and weak, we are strong unexpected by the power and grace of the Almighty God. (2 Cor.1-10; Ps.33.18)

4. Let us humble ourselves under the mighty hand of God, so that his will and purpose may be fulfilled in our lives and work. (1 Pet.5.6-11)   Amen!

SERMON NO.192/C-63

Twenty –fourth Sunday After Pentecost

M/EW   *Scripture Readings:*
                Ps .16   1 Cor.15.12-26
                Dan . 12.1-3   Lk.20.27-40

Theme: Resurrection and the life of the world to come

Sermon Outline:

1. Daniel saw the vision of the condemnation of the wicked and salvation of the righteous at the end. (Dan .12.1-3)

2. Jesus taught that there is no marriage in heaven, and the sons of resurrection shall be like the angels in the world to come. (Lk.20.27-40)

3. St.Paul taught that Christ is risen as the first fruit among the dead, and the children of God shall be risen like him at the end. (1 Cor.15.12ff; 1 Thess.4.14-16; Ps.16.10)

4. Let us remain prepared for the Day of the Lord to be risen from among the dead, and enjoy eternal life in heaven. (Phil.1.9-11; Col.3.1-4; Rev.3.19-22)   Amen!

SERMON NO.193/C-64

Twenty- fourth Sunday After Pentecost

M /EW   *Scriptures Readings:*
                Ps.69.1-18   2 Cor.4.7-18
                Mic.7.1-10a   Lk.21.5-19

Theme: God upholds those who suffer for his sake

Sermon Outline:

1. The end time shall be extremely troublesome, but the Lord will save his people. (Mic.7.1-10a; Lk.21.5-19)

2. There shall be severe trials and tribulations for the people of God, but risen Lord shall give life and shall save his people. (2 Cor.4.7-18; Ps.69)

3. Let us be faithful to the Lord and to one another even in the days of tribulations, and the Saviour Lord is faithful to save us . (2 Tim.2.11-13) Amen!

SERMON NO.194/C-65

Twenty-sixth Sunday After Pentecost

M/EW   *Scripture Readings:*

Ps.119.17-32   Heb.6.1-12

Ezra 8.15a, 21-32   Lk.9.57-52

Theme: Whole-hearted service to God

Sermon Outline:

1. Ezra's leadership was an example of whole-hearted service to God. (Ezra 8.15a, 21-320

2. God looks for people who can work for him with steadfastness and perseverance. (Lk.9.57-62)

3. Those who betray and act unrighteously are not fit for God's work. (Heb.6.1-12)

4. Let us serve the Lord whole-heartedly, receive his blessings and be his witnesses. Amen!

SERMON NO.195/C-66

Twenty-seventh and
Last Sunday After Pentecost

M/EW   *Scripture Readings:*

Ps.74   Phil.3.17-4.1

Is.28.14-17   Lk.23.32-43

Theme: The kingly glory of Jesus on the Cross

Sermon Outline:

1. The Lord Jesus graciously prayed to the Father to forgive his enemies who crucified him. (L.k.23.32-43)

2. The Lord authoritatively invited the repentant criminal to paradise. (Lk.23.43)

3. Jesus' crucifixion and resurrection have been the goal of our Christian life to press on. (Phil.3.17-4.1, 1 Cor.1.8; 15.45)

4. Jesus, on the cross, demonstrated as the Son of God and the eternal King, as he had confessed before Pilate in his trial. (L.k.22.70; Jn.18.37)

5. The Lord Jesus is the King, and the King for ever! Let us praise Him, and adore His holy and saving name. Halleluyah. Amen!

www.ingramcontent.com/pod-product-compliance
Lightning Source LLC
LaVergne TN
LVHW091512170726
843492LV00001B/457